John Helvi T3-BNK-456

INDIANA'S
BELIEVE IT
OR NOT

INDIANA'S
BELIEVE IT
OR NOT

FRED D. CAVINDER

■

INDIANA UNIVERSITY PRESS
BLOOMINGTON & INDIANAPOLIS

© 1990 by Fred D. Cavinder

All rights reserved

No part of this book may be reproduced or utilized in any form or by any means, electronic or mechanical, including photocopying and recording, or by any information storage and retrieval system, without permission in writing from the publisher. The Association of American University Presses' Resolution on Permissions constitutes the only exception to this prohibition.

The paper used in this publication meets the minimum requirements of American National Standard for Information Sciences— Permanence of Paper for Printed Library Materials, ANSI Z39.48-1984.

∞

Manufactured in the United States of America

Library of Congress Cataloging-in-Publication Data

Cavinder, Fred D.
    Indiana's believe it or not / Fred D. Cavinder.
        p.   cm.
    ISBN 0-253-31329-5 (alk. paper). — ISBN 0-253-20586-7 (pbk. : alk. paper)
        1. Indiana—Miscellanea.   2. Curiosities and wonders—Indiana.
I. Title.
F526.5.C37   1990
977.2—dc20   89-46005
                                                                    CIP

1 2 3 4 5   94 93 92 91 90

Contents

XI INTRODUCTION
1 THE BOY WHO WANTED TO BE BURIED
1 THE KREMLIN CONNECTION
2 THE OHIO RIVER TURNAROUND
2 ABUZZ IN THE BOG
3 THE MOTHER OF STREAMS
4 THE GHOST STREAM
5 IRONPLATED WELSHMEN
5 FABULOUS FLOW
6 JOLTED INTO ACTION
7 DUAL DUELS
8 THE GRASS IS ALWAYS BLUER
9 PORTRAIT OF THE ARTIST'S FATHER
10 THE YEAR WITHOUT A SUMMER
11 IN THE KEY OF STRANGE
12 THE DEVIL SPIRIT
14 THE COUNTY THAT DISAPPEARED
15 THE LEGENDARY BEAR WOMAN
17 HARRIET, TOM, AND ELIZA
19 PASSING THE WORD
20 A SPEL OF REFORMASHUN
21 CHINA AND THE MARTIN DYNASTY
22 THE ALMOST PRESIDENT

23 THE SOULE OF GREELEY
24 MARK OF THE HUNTER
24 THIS GUN FOR HIRE
25 GOING WHOLE HOG
26 THE UNHAPPY WANDERER
28 A MAN WHO . . . AND ANOTHER MAN WHO . . . AND . . .
29 READING, WRITING, AND STAGE FRIGHT
30 BOGGSTOWN GOES SOUTH
32 THE LADY ON THE FRONT LINES
34 CRADLE OF COMMANDERS
35 THE GAT WITH A MISSION
37 COWED AT VERNON
38 DESERTION AND DISGRACE
39 OFF THE WALL EDITION
40 HOOSIERS AWEIGH
41 START THE PRESSES
43 THE ASSASSINATION ASSEMBLAGE
45 COURTHOUSE TREE-TOP TALL
47 THE GIRL WHO WASN'T THERE
49 THE CIRCUS'S GREATEST COUP
50 BURNING DESIRE TO DIE
51 ATTRACTIVE WATER
52 THE ONE AND ONLY CURVE-BALL PITCHER
53 UNEASY RESTS THE HEAD OF STATE
55 STRETCH, THE MOUND BUILDER
56 BEDROCK IMAGINATION
58 THE DOME THAT DAUNTS SCIENCE
58 FROM A RELIABLE SOURCE . . .

59   THE BENEFACTOR OF BOOKS
60   ALL SHIPS ABOARD
61   NEED A BODY CRY
62   INDIANA'S PHARAOH
62   THE DESPERATE DESIGNER
64   KNOWING BEANS ABOUT IT
64   CORN ON THE CURRENT
65   HARRISON THE FLAG WAVER
67   AT GRAMMAR HE DECLINED
68   THE KOUTS BOUT
69   HE RODE FOR A FALL
70   THE BIGGER THEY COME
75   WAKE-A-BYE JONES
77   SIGHT VERSUS INSIGHT
78   PREACHING POWER
79   FROM HORSEHIDE TO COWBOYS
80   THE HORSE SENSE THAT FALTERED
83   HAPPY—NOT SO FAST—BIRTHDAY
83   THE HANGING JUDGMENT
85   PREGNANT WITH PROMISE
86   FINGERS ENOUGH
88   THE MOSQUITO MARTYR
89   MOTHER'S INITIAL HELPER
90   DEAD CENTER IN THE ROAD
92   WHEN SMOKING CAUSED SPARKS
93   QUIET PLEASE, THIS IS AN ELECTION
94   LEWDNESS AND A "G" STRING
95   LITTLE BIG-LEAGUE TOWN
96   BALLOONING

98   PRISON INSIDE AND OUTSIDE

100   CASH ON THE COB

100   WORLD SERIES WONDER

101   GIVING IT THE GAS

103   JUDAH GOES TO THE MOVIES

105   A CONGRESSMAN AND HIS DOG

107   A TIP OF THE HAT TO . . .

107   HERE'S TO THE HEAT

109   LUMBERING GIANTS

112   PLANTED THEN, DUG LATER

113   PAINTING BY NUMBERS

115   WHAT'S IN A NAME?

115   THE DUNES FLOWER CHILD

118   THE CENTER WHO CARRIED HIS LOAD

119   VICTIM AND SURVIVOR

120   IMMOVABLE FORCE, IRRESISTIBLE OBJECT

120   HOT TIME IN THE OLD STATE

121   THE UP AND DOWN TOUCHDOWN

122   REACH OUT AND SHIFT SOMEONE

125   DEAD MEN HAVE TALES

126   HUSKING CORN FOR 200,000 EARS

127   IT WAS HIS FUNERAL

128   CALIGULA, IL DUCE, AND A HOOSIER

129   ANIMAL ANOMALIES

130   INFANTILE INCIDENTS

131   THE BROTHERS OF STONE

132   MUSIC TO MILK BY

132   WANTED: ONE MODEL

133   THE VILLAGE THAT VANISHED

135 ODON'S HOME FIRES BURNING
136 THE ATTACK BLIMP
137 BITTEN BY FAME
139 HORSE SENSE
140 A SALUTE TO THE KERNEL
141 RING AROUND THE COMMODE
142 NO BONES ABOUT IT
143 TEST CASE FOR AUCTIONEERS
145 EXECUTION BY SURGERY
146 THE FALL AND RISE OF ROGER REYNOLDS
147 THE POSTER THAT SHOULDN'T HAVE BEEN
148 MARJORIE'S MILLIONS
150 A HOME THAT'S QUITE A HOUSE
152 MOTHER PLAYED BASKETBALL
153 FISH STORIES
154 WETTING DAY
155 TWO BY TWO BY TWO
156 A LITTLE SOAP NEVER HURT
156 IN THE CHIPS
157 BEATING THE ODDS

MY mother, who lived ninety-one years as a Hoosier, used an expression common to people of her era which was a perfect response to a startling announcement.

"Will wonders never cease?" she used to say.

The phrase served to express genuine amazement and was equally suitable, with proper inflection, for mockery. But either way, she was right; wonders probably never will cease.

The tall story, which was almost an art form, a method of entertainment in pioneer days, has never lost its charm for Hoosiers. Tall accomplishments—the stuff to provoke disbelief—still enthrall audiences.

Indiana's past and present are dotted with examples that can raise the eyebrows of a Hoosier, who doesn't easily arch a brow. Outsiders might say in bewilderment, "A Hoosier did that?" But Indianans have come to take the stand-out quality of the state almost for granted. They know Hoosiers are on top of so many heaps, have led in so many fields, been out ahead of the competition in so many ways that to say, for instance, that Jerry Harkness was playing for a Hoosier team, the Indiana Pacers, when he scored with a shot ninety-two feet from the basket is considered stating the obvious.

Robert L. Ripley's "Believe It or Not," being carried on posthumously, made note of Harkness's feat with a mention in April 1968, but to Hoosiers, as is so often the case, it was old news.

The Indiana attitude works both ways. If Hoosiers are blasé about the bizarre, the bewildering, and the by-gosh, they are equally confident in their ability to do the impossible, the improbable, and the impressionable.

How else can you account for Col. Hugh McGary founding an Indiana city in 1812, when the state was a wilderness and travel was a struggle, just to be closer to his in-laws? The concept itself is pure early Hoosier. McGary lived west of what is now Princeton. His wife's relatives lived at Henderson (then called Red Banks), Kentucky, a trip of some thirty miles. By moving to the Ohio River and starting a ferry, McGary cut down on reunion travel time and incidentally started the village that became Evansville.

McGary was a known historical figure. Another Hoosier, the "meanest man in the world," a Noble Countian of bygone times, remains nameless, perhaps apocryphal, because his actions were too weird to be attributed to a real person. He divorced his wife, this mean fellow, and remarried. But his ex-wife, unable to make ends meet, entered the county poor asylum in the days when "pauper sales" were held. Sold to the highest bidder, the inmates of the poor house were forced to work for the new master, enslaved for their keep.

You guessed it; the mean Hoosier man bought back his own wife and put her to doing the heavy housework for his new mate. Believe that or not.

Indiana is not without the standard classic events to which Ripley eagerly applied pen during the halcyon days of his reign as America's sideshow king. His biographers have pointed out that Ripley himself was a genuine wonder. Self-taught, ill-educated, everything Ripley learned *was* unbelievable to him. He accepted anything as authentic which could be found in print, and he loved to fool readers by careful omission.

Sometimes his bizarre items sounded a bit like comedy

repartee. "My grandmother lived to be eighty-five and never used glasses," is what Ripley might report. What he would leave unsaid is: "She drank straight from the bottle."

Indiana can join such a freakiness parade.

In February 1934, a needle one-and-one-half inches long was removed from the arm of I. A. Defenbaugh of Greenfield, thirty-four years after he had swallowed it.

Winfield T. Durbin, later to be governor of Indiana, was one of seven brothers who enlisted in the Union Army on the same day.

At Owensville, claimed Frank Edwards, a TV commentator who for years was king of oddities in Indiana, the message "Remember Pearl Harbor" appeared on the sidewalks—two years before the Japanese attacked Pearl Harbor in 1941.

Michael Jackson, famed singer from Gary, offered a large sum of money to buy the skeleton of John Merrick, the Elephant Man, whose remains have been preserved in a London medical college.

While these are great barroom items, there are many other less well known but equally fascinating Indiana stories which you'll encounter here: stories of Hoosiers whose weight made them circus personalities, sports figures who did the improbable, eerie tales involving graves and those in them—or out of them, psychic animals, personalities who left an imprint on Indiana because of their blend of sheer determination and off-beat ambition.

The stories in this book have been extracted from newspaper files, local and state historical books, occasionally from contemporary headlines. No doubt the world has seen stranger events and more unusual people. But, considering that the boundaries of Indiana are the restrictions of imagination in these odd stories, they represent a fair cross-section of Hoosier shocks and tingles.

It is only a cross-section, however. There are no doubt

many more tales in the annals of *Indiana's Believe It or Not*. Because what Robert Ripley said and what my mother knew years ago still applies: "The supply is really inexhaustible, isn't it?"

INDIANA'S
BELIEVE IT
OR NOT

THE BOY WHO WANTED TO BE BURIED ■

Among Indiana stories of ghostly suspense, perhaps the most bizarre is the case of the dead youth who remained unburied until his spirit told his mother it was time to put him to rest.

The place was Medora, the site, Dr. Creed Taylor Wilson's dream home, built a few miles west of town in 1848 along what later became Indiana 50.

Aesop C. Wilson, the youngest child of the doctor and his wife, died of typhoid fever in a camp in Missouri in 1861 while serving with Indiana Vol., Co. B., 22nd Regiment in the Civil War. The body was shipped home in 1862. The boy's mother had it sealed in charcoal in a lead coffin and placed in an upstairs hallway by a large front window. There she would often sit, rocking back and forth, talking earnestly to her lost boy or knitting and mending.

Dr. Wilson, who had tried without success to get his wife to bury the body, finally called on spiritualists from Louisville, Kentucky. In a session at the Wilson home, the voice of the dead boy was heard imploring his mother to bury his body in a small grove of cedars just north of the house.

His wishes were followed at once—a case of a voice which might be said to have come from the grave before its body was in it.

THE KREMLIN CONNECTION ■

Paper coal, a rare relic of the coal age, is composed of the waxy coatings of ancient leaves and twigs. Unlike the denser true coal, it is light and flaky, resembling scorched paper. Paper coal has been found in the Moscow Basin in Central Russia, and in only one other place in the world—Parke County, Indiana. Indiana's paper coal consists mostly of fragments of seed ferns, extinct for more than 200 million years, experts say.

Existence of the fragile cuticles indicates that they were deposited in quiet lagoons. Oxidation of the original plant material has left behind the more resistant cuticles, a curious link between Indiana and Russia.

■ THE OHIO RIVER TURNAROUND

Many years ago, before the great glacier worked its modifications on Indiana, the river along what is now the Indiana-Kentucky border flowed northeastward—the opposite direction from its course today.

What was known as the Kentucky River flowed from Indiana into west-central Ohio and joined the Teays River, which flowed west. The Teays crossed Indiana north of Lafayette.

The Ohio River of today was formed when the glacier blocked the drainageway of the Kentucky, causing it to form into a pond. This contained water crossed a divide near Madison into a small tributary of the Salt River. This river, aided by water from the melting glacier, cut through the land and helped to form the Ohio River as we now know it—flowing southwestward.

The glacier meanwhile buried the valley of the Teays River, concealing from Hoosiers of today the river turnaround of ancient times.

■ ABUZZ IN THE BOG

At Pinhook Bog in northwest LaPorte County, a mosquito joins forces with a plant to form one of the rarest associations in Indiana's outdoor world.

The mosquito is *Wyoemyia smithii*, one of the most specialized of the more than fifty types of mosquitoes found in Indiana. It lives only in bogs, making its known habitats Pinhook Bog and possibly Cowles Bog, also in LaPorte County.

The mosquito's restriction to bogs is due to its link with the pitcher plant, which grows only in bogs.

Although the pitcher plant eats all other insects, it provides a home for the *Wyoemyia smithii* mosquito, letting the larvae coexist with the very juices which bring an end to other insects.

The pitcher plant captures prey with downward-slanting bristles that prevent an exploring insect from crawling out. Once the bug reaches the fluid in the plant, it is dissolved and digested. Yet the *Wyoemyia smithii* thrives in this atmosphere, making it not only the rarest mosquito in Indiana's few bogs, but also the insect with the most dangerous home.

THE MOTHER OF STREAMS ■

Lots of water flows out of Randolph County. The number of rivers that originate in and immediately around this square county which abuts the Ohio state line surpasses any other single spot of its size in the state. Within a circle extending only a few miles beyond Randolph County are the sources of twelve rivers, nine major water systems, and three streams barely qualified as rivers.

Streams spawned in Randolph County eventually gather water from seventy-eight of the ninety-two counties in Indiana and several counties in southwestern Ohio.

The reason is simple; Randolph is the state's highest county. More unusual is that a system of moraines, ridges of earth and stone deposited by the great glacier, form barriers which prevent headwaters from joining into a single river. Instead, the water scurries in all directions.

Streams beginning in Randolph County are the West Fork of White River, the West Fork of Whitewater, Greenville Creek, Dismal Creek, and Little Mississinewa River. Streams that begin just outside the county include the Salamonie River and Little Salamonie River, Mississinewa River, Wabash River, Stillwater River, East Fork of Whitewater River, Blue River, Flat Rock River, and Little White River.

■ THE GHOST STREAM

Indiana's deepest river is the Lost River, in which divers have descended to a depth of 165 feet.

Lost River gets its name because a quarter of its 85-mile length is underground. The disappearing act is blamed on a series of sinkholes so numerous that in one square mile 1,022 have been counted.

Where the river rises again from the earth, near Orangeville in northwestern Orange County, it produces the third largest spring in Indiana, and the deepest. Here divers have gone 165 feet down one nearly vertical slot which meets a horizontal conduit at the bottom, believed to be the underground channel of the stream.

Two sinkholes by which Lost River seeks its underground course are National Natural Landmarks—Tolliver Swallowhole and Wesley Chapel Gulf, which covers 8.3 acres, a sort of box canyon in which the river makes a brief surface appearance.

Lost River begins in western Washington County. It flows like a normal river, then disappears, leaving a dry stream bed. The stream passes through Orange County to the Orangeville Rise. Then it flows on the surface again in southern Martin County, finally reaching the East Fork of White River.

The estimated twenty-three miles of the stream that

are invisible can be accounted a river mystery unsurpassed anywhere in the world.

Ironplated Welshmen ■

Archeologists say that a "Stone Fort" and embankments near Charlestown are the work of Mound Builders known to have been in Indiana in very early times.

But some Hoosiers declare that the stone and earth were the work of twelfth-century Welshmen, one of whom left behind a suit of armor. It was found on the banks of the Ohio River near Jeffersonville in 1799, legend insists, made of brass, bearing a Welsh coat-of-arms, the "Mermaid and the Harp," with a Latin inscription meaning "Virtuous deeds merit their just reward."

Tradition says that during contention among seventeen sons as to who would succeed the Prince of Wales in 1167, one son, Madoc, sailed west to seek his fortune and reached the Ohio near Jeffersonville. There he and his men lived.

George Rogers Clark said Indians told him of a battle at the Falls of the Ohio between Indians and a "strange race." Explorer George Catlin told of encountering Indians whose dialect included occasional Welsh words, and who used basket boats like those used by the Welsh.

The armor, the most striking relic of that legendary time, is gone, but the tale persists against all attackers.

Fabulous Flow ■

The largest spring in Indiana produces enough water to serve the average Hoosier town of 12,000 people.

Harrison Spring, just north of White Cloud in Harrison County, covers about 800 square feet to a depth of thirty-five feet and produces a minimum of 3 million gallons a day. During heavy rains the spring's output is as much as ten times normal.

Corydon, the closest town of any size to the spring, has considered seeking it as a water source. State figures show that the spring could supply three times the water needed by Corydon, whose 4,500 water users require only about 750,000 gallons a day.

Now owned by Robert Rosenbarger, the spring once was part of the farm of William Henry Harrison, governor of the Indiana Territory from 1800 to 1812. Near the spring in 1807 Harrison constructed a sawmill and gristmill, one of the first water-powered mills in the state.

Today, instead of being used by any town, Harrison Spring overflows into an outlet which travels about half a mile to Blue River.

■ JOLTED INTO ACTION

Little Cedar Grove Baptist Church near Brookville owes its existence to an earthquake.

The church had been formed in 1806, but pioneers procrastinated in erecting a building until 1811.

In December of that year an earthquake hit the Midwest and shocks continued into the next year. According to some observers, the earthquake was taken as a warning that it was time to get on with God's work.

Rev. Allen Wiley, a Methodist circuit rider, wrote of it this way, taking into account denominational differences: "The people ran to and fro, called for prayer meeting, exhorted each other to good deeds and repented of their sins as if Judgment Day was at hand. Then they met in solemn conclave and made a covenant with the Almighty that if He would send no more earthquakes, they would build Him a church."

Little Cedar Grove Baptist Church (1812) was built because of an earthquake. The small holes at second-floor level were gun ports, intended for defense against possible Indian attacks in the era just before Indiana became a state. (Photo by the author)

Completed August 1, 1812, Little Cedar Grove Baptist Church is the oldest in Indiana still on its original foundation, from which it'never has been stirred by quakes or tremors.

Dual Duels ■

The duel between Capt. Parmenas Beckes and Dr. Edward Scull was to be expected in an era when dueling, although illegal, commonly served to settle affairs of honor. But when a second duel resulted in the same ironic outcome, an eerie touch of drama was added, along with a twist of macabre whimsy.

Beckes and Scull both had served at the Battle of Tippecanoe and both were residents of Vincennes, where Dr. Scull had a medical practice. He also had an acquaintance with Beckes's stepdaughter.

Dr. Scull was accused of besmirching the honor of the girl, a charge he denied. When he refused to marry her, Beckes sought a duel. The site of the encounter in July 1813 was across the Wabash River from Vincennes and downstream a short distance.

At the command to fire, Scull deliberately shot into the air. Beckes, perhaps unnerved by his rage, shot wide and Scull considered the affair ended. Not so, cried Beckes. "We will shoot until sundown or until one of us falls."

Dr. Scull's second shot struck Beckes in the side; he died within minutes.

Three months later, after Scull had sold his practice and left town, his second in the duel, Lt. Thomas H. Richardson, challenged a young Vincennes citizen to a duel. Irwin Wallace had charged that Beckes's death had been murder. Richardson objected and the pair went to the same spot where the earlier duel had been fought. The result was the same. The challenger, Richardson, died on the second shot, just as the challenger had in the first duel.

In the pair of duels, the same guns were used, at the same place. Both victims were struck in the right side, both died immediately, and both were buried with military honors in the same cemetery.

■ THE GRASS IS ALWAYS BLUER

The bluegrass that provided a descriptive name for the state of Kentucky actually came from Indiana. At least, if you can believe Kentucky patriot Henry Clay it did.

He said soldiers from Kentucky obtained bluegrass

seed when they fought Indians along the Wabash River from their station at old Fort Harrison, near Terre Haute. The fort was constructed to protect settlers from warriors of Tecumseh, an Indian leader during Indiana's pre-statehood days.

Clay's explanation was given to Henry S. Lane of Crawfordsville and Col. Thomas Dowling of Terre Haute when they visited Clay's Kentucky home, Ashland, and asked for some seeds to take back to Indiana.

The Terre Haute area, especially Putnam County, was in fact noted for its bluegrass in pioneer days. A limestone base with a superstratum of clay was said to be a natural habitat for the plant.

That it prompted early cattlemen to import herds to Putnam County to thrive on the bluegrass merely supports Clay's contention that Kentuckians took it south with them so their steeds could continue to enjoy the forage they had grazed upon at Fort Harrison.

Portrait of the Artist's Father ■

Who is the most forgotten Hoosier? A good candidate is Whistler's father.

George Whistler, father of artist James A. McNeill Whistler, painter of the world-famous portrait of his mother, was born inside the stockade at Fort Wayne. His father, Maj. John Whistler, was stockade commandant. George Whistler was graduated from the United States Military Academy in 1819 and taught there before becoming a civil engineer.

He worked on a survey of the international boundary between Lake Superior and Lake of the Woods, aided in building the Baltimore & Ohio Railroad in 1828, and inspected railroads in England.

Russia called on his expertise. In 1844 he began supervising construction of 420 miles of rails connecting St. Petersburg and Moscow, a seven-year project which he finished in six years. Then he helped build rolling stock for the Russians, who honored him with a medal.

In 1849 he was struck down by cholera.

He never was painted by his son and never gained the immortality achieved by his wife through "Arrangement in Gray and Black," the formal title of the painting that came to be known as "Whistler's Mother." In fact, it's a safe trivia bet that most people have forgotten, if they ever knew, that George Whistler was born a Hoosier.

■ THE YEAR WITHOUT A SUMMER

In 1816 Hoosiers didn't suffer from heat during the summer. They froze.

Ice, snow, and sleet destroyed crops for both white men and Indians in what was soon to be the state of Indiana. In April, spring seemed to be arriving as usual. But ice and snow at the end of the month destroyed crops. New seedlings in May never had a chance. Snow or sleet fell during seventeen days in May. Snow in June finished off any surviving crops, blackened leaves on trees, and froze many livestock.

The estimated 60,000 Indiana pioneers began to take seriously predictions of snow in July by the *Old New England Farmer's Almanack and Register*. July 4 brought bitter weather. During the first week of July the upper 1,000 miles of what is now the United States suffered freezing temperatures.

August was worse. Snow, frost, and blizzards hit. Ice covered much of the nation. Indiana fruit trees were destroyed. Corn was killed repeatedly until it was too late to replant. Only wilderness plants, hardier than hybrid crops, survived.

Beset by inflation, Hoosiers turned to the wilderness for food. Raccoons and groundhogs became standard vittles. Passenger pigeons replaced poultry on the table. The woods were searched for wild sweet potatoes, jack-in-the-pulpit bulbs, and wild onions.

The six years from 1812 to 1817 were tough, with unusual cold all over the world. But never was Indiana's crop-growing season as frigid as during 1816—the year without a summer.

IN THE KEY OF STRANGE ◼

The first known piano in Indiana was played by a tragic musician.

Mary Wright arrived at Vevay with her parents, an aristocratic but impoverished couple from England who had fled to the new land to escape the pain of economic and social reverses. They brought by flatboat a piano made by Muzio Clementi of Italy.

Not the least of unpleasant memories for Mary was her desertion by her English fiancé. Heartbroken, she was further bewildered by the wild, rough country around Vevay in 1817. The piano was her only solace.

She spent all the daylight hours in her room on the second floor of the family's rough log cabin, going out only to wander in the moonlight. But once a week, wearing a splendid dress and jewels, she would descend the ladder from her room, play her repertoire without a word, and disappear again upstairs.

The routine continued for forty years. The songs never varied, the program never expanded, the piano was never tuned. Mary Wright was found dead in her room in 1874 when she was eighty-two. The piano found its way somehow to an abandoned building where it was discovered years later and placed in the Switzerland County Historical Society Museum.

For forty years Mary Wright played through her bizarre and plaintive repertoire on this piano, now preserved in the Switzerland County Historical Society Museum at Vevay. (Photo by the author)

■ THE DEVIL SPIRIT

Indiana may not have a Loch Ness, but it has had its own monster, surprisingly similar to the fabled beast in Scotland which has intrigued observers for centuries.

The Indiana monster goes back to before the time settlers arrived at Lake Manitou near Kewanna. Members of a local Indian tribe reported a monster serpent with a scaly tail in the lake. They called it Manitou, meaning spirit.

During construction of a corn mill for the Potawatomis in 1827, sightings of the beast made it difficult for the surveyor to keep helpers on the payroll, local historians reported. The area's first blacksmith described the monster like this: "The head being about three feet across the frontal bone and having something of the contour of a beef's head, but the neck tapering and having the character of the serpent; color dingy with large yellow spots."

In 1838 men told the *Logansport Telegraph* of seeing something sixty feet long in the lake. Using their descriptions, George Winter, noted painter of Indians near Kewanna, sketched his conception of the monster for the newspaper.

Some scoffed at further sightings, and some believed that in 1849, when a huge buffalo carp was caught in the lake, the monster had been bested. The carp's thirty-pound head was exhibited at Logansport.

Indiana artist George Winter's watercolor sketch of the Manitou monster, based on reports of an 1838 sighting, showed a suggestion for catching the monster. (Tippecanoe County Historical Assn. Gift of Mrs. Cable B. Ball)

But monster stories would not be stilled. In 1881 Margaret Holmes published a romantic novel titled *Manitou* in which a state senator is chased by the monster.

In 1888 a 116-pound spoonbill catfish was caught by four fishermen, who exhibited it in a horse trough at the county courthouse for a week, charging viewers ten cents for a peek at the "monster." Then the spoonbill played yet another week at Logansport. By this time near death, the fish was dressed and sold at ten cents a pound.

In recent years talk of the Manitou monster has waned, but, like its Loch Ness counterpart, nobody can foretell when it may appear again, to bring to life the terrifying portrait painted by George Winter.

■ THE COUNTY THAT DISAPPEARED

In 1835 Newton County existed on a map as a large section of land in northwest Indiana. It had no government, only geographic boundaries established by the state legislature. But four years later it had vanished.

The legislature had created Newton to include what are now southern portions of Lake and Porter counties and the northern halves of what are Jasper and Newton counties today.

One by one Newton's neighboring counties organized, and each claimed some territory from Newton. In 1839 when Jasper became a county it claimed all that was left of the original Newton County territory.

Newton had disappeared before it even officially became a county.

Farmers near Morocco, fearful that their views would be ignored at the distant Jasper County seat, petitioned to reorganize the county, a plea which was eventually approved by the Indiana Supreme Court.

Present boundaries were established in 1860, and

Newton County, which once had vanished, officially reappeared as the last county organized in Indiana.

THE LEGENDARY BEAR WOMAN ∎

Frances Slocum's story of life with the Indians was so bizarre, even in the 1830s with Indians still present and conflict with them fresh in the minds of Indiana settlers, that it was set aside for another two years as too improbable.

But once verified, the saga, more than sixty years in the making, became so compelling it became trans-

Frances Slocum, "Litttle Bear Woman" (1772–1847), and her daughters; watercolor by George Winter. (Tippecanoe County Historical Assn. Gift of Mrs. Cable G. Ball)

formed into a legend. In the years since, Frances Slocum's life never has lost its allure for Hoosiers. She became the wife of a chieftain; she became so thoroughly Indian that she concealed her real identity until faced with mortality. But even in the twilight of her years, when the white world beckoned, she could not rejoin it.

Frances came from Quakers in Pennsylvania. The Delawares honored the Quakers' pacifism and exempted them from the fighting in the late 1770s. But when one of Frances's brothers took up arms during an attack in July 1778 near Wilkes-Barre, the Slocums lost their immunity from attack. Later that year six-year-old Frances Slocum was carried away by raiding Indians. Her father was killed in the fields in a second attack. Her mother, convinced Frances was alive, began a search for the girl which she didn't abandon until 1826.

No trace was found until 1835 when trader George Washington Ewing visited Indians living near Peru. He suspected his hostess was white and that she had something to confide. Eventually she told Ewing of her Pennsylvania background, her father named Slocum, who wore a broad-brimmed hat, and her seizure by the Indians. Named Maconaqua (meaning Little Bear Woman) because of her strength, she had been reared by a chief named Tuck Horse. Her travels with the Indians led to Indiana.

She had wed Shepocanah, a young Miami chief she had nursed to health from a wound. Pushed by civilization, Shepocanah moved away from Fort Wayne. When age and deafness caused him to resign as a chief, he had moved to the banks of the Mississinewa River and built a settlement for his family. After she was dead—an event she expected soon—Ewing might reveal her real identity, the woman told him.

Ewing wrote a letter detailing the woman's story to the postmaster at Lancaster, Pennsylvania, hoping someone in that Quaker region might identify the white woman. Incredulous, Mrs. Mary Dickson, the Lancaster postmaster, put the letter aside. It was found two years later by the new postmaster, John Forney, who gave it to the *Lancaster Intelligencer,* thinking the tale would interest newspaper readers.

Joseph Slocum, a brother of Frances, saw the story and took his brother Isaac and sister Mary to visit Frances on September 21, 1837. They identified her by her hair, scars, and a missing finger, which had been cut off in a blacksmith shop accident. Frances rejected appeals to return to Pennsylvania. She said she was like an old tree that would die if transplanted.

In 1847 (her premonition of death had been premature) Frances developed a fever after joining in a tribal dance of thanksgiving to welcome spring. She died March 9, 1847, at the age of seventy-four. As agreed, she was given a Christian funeral and buried on a hill near her home, the site marked by a white flag, which Frances had requested so the Great Spirit would not forget her.

She didn't know she would be remembered with memorials all the way from Wilkes-Barre, where she was captured, to Indiana, where she revealed one of the strangest tales in Hoosier Indian lore.

HARRIET, TOM, AND ELIZA ■

A black family in Indianapolis provided the real-life inspiration for Uncle Tom and his family, characters made famous by Harriet Beecher Stowe in *Uncle Tom's Cabin.*

And Eliza, whose flight across an icy river was one of the highlights of the book, was in real life Eliza Harris of Kentucky, who reached safety across the frozen Ohio River and fled to Jay County.

How Mrs. (Calvin E.) Stowe learned of Eliza's adventure is uncertain, but her visits to the real-life Uncle Tom were well documented. In the 1840s Mrs. Stowe, wife of a professor at Cincinnati's Lane Theological Seminary, spent much time in Indianapolis visiting her brother, the Rev. Henry Ward Beecher, pastor of the Second Presbyterian Church. She also often visited Tom Magruder, who lived at Noble and Market streets with his wife, daughter, a son named Mose, and a young Negro named Pete who was a permanent roomer.

Observers said Mrs. Stowe took notebook and pencil on her visits, evidently making notes. When her book appeared in 1852 to rock the nation, the fictional people around Uncle Tom's cabin closely matched the real people around Tom Magruder's Indianapolis cabin.

Eliza was owned by a Kentuckian; although he was kind, economics forced him to sell his slaves and Eliza feared she and her baby might be separated. She fled. Her path took her across the Ohio River, and her trail from there to safety in Canada was documented by the famed Indiana underground railroad conductor Levi Coffin of Fountain City.

Coffin recalled that Eliza had found safety in the home of Mrs. Rachel Sullivan two miles north of Pennville near the village of Balbec. In 1854, Coffin stated, he visited Eliza, who was living in safety near Chatham, Ontario.

Pennville residents once erected a monument at the site of Mrs. Sullivan's cabin bearing a tablet which read: "A station on the underground railroad. Tradition says Eliza Harris of Uncle Tom's Cabin fame rested here in her flight to Canada."

The real Uncle Tom died peacefully in bed on Washington's birthday, 1857.

"Uncle Tom's Cabin" created its own monument in literature, of course, even if Indiana perhaps didn't get the credit it deserved for providing the dramatic scenarios.

A Hoosier girl's words were the first sent on the telegraph because she was the one to bring inventor Samuel F. B. Morse the good news that Congress had come through with the money.

Her name was Ann Ellsworth. She lived at 7th and South streets in Lafayette, but she was in Washington that day in 1843 because her father, Henry L. Ellsworth, was commissioner of patents. Ellsworth was a friend of Morse, who had spent all of March 4 in frustration because it appeared that the Senate would adjourn before appropriating $30,000 for completion of the telegraph system Morse had invented.

Morse went to bed that night believing that the money bill had died and his hopes along with it. But in the morning Ann Ellsworth arrived and offered him congratulations on passage of the bill.

"Father was there at the adjournment at midnight," she told the disbelieving inventor, "and saw the president put his name to your bill, and I asked father if I might come and tell you and he gave me leave. Am I the first to tell you?"

Indeed she was, and, as a reward, Morse vowed that when the line was completed between Washington and Baltimore, Ann Ellsworth should compose the first dispatch.

On May 24, 1844, when a group assembled in the United States Supreme Court chambers to witness the first test of the telegraph, they heard the words chosen by her, the last phrase of the twenty-third verse of the twenty-third chapter of Numbers: "What hath God wrought?"

■ A Spel of Reformashun

You might say William C. Talcott had a way with words.

He devised a method of spelling which found few disciples in the 1840s. However, pupils today learn to read using the Initial Teaching Alphabet (ITA) before reverting to the conventional system of spelling. The fact that ITA bears some resemblances to Talcott's phonetic alphabet shows how far he was ahead of his times.

Talcott, a resident of Valparaiso, called his spelling phonotypy. As early as 1843 he urged subscribers to his newspaper, which evolved into today's *Vidette-Messenger,* to adopt his method. It would reduce necessary schooling by two years, Talcott contended, and would save America at least $3 million a day—at 1840s prices—through savings in time, printing space and instructional expenses.

Talcott assigned a single sound to each letter. Uniformity of sound and spelling in his system resulted in words like "erly" for "early." To make the system work, Talcott eliminated K, Q, and X from the alphabet, and added letters, resulting in a 39-letter alphabet. He added such things as a double U for the "oo" sound and a letter that looked like an inverted question mark for the "th" sound.

The phonetic alphabet was not Talcott's only attempt at reformation. He also pushed for changes as an attorney, judge, teacher, minister, author, publisher, surveyor, sociologist, and advocate of racial equality and equal rights for women. He reduced his religious philosophy to the Golden Rule after exploring Presbyterianism and the Universalist Church. He founded a commune, which failed after two years, and he advocated a single legislative body for the state and replacement of state regulations with national laws.

Although most of his reforms vanished into history,

his views on women's rights and phonetic spelling survive. Women's rights were outlined in rhyme in his book, *Doktrin and Practis,* published in 1889, and his phonetic spelling survives on his tombstone at Valparaiso. The inscription, devised by Talcott before his death, says in part:

"In memori uv Wm. C. Tolkut ho woz born Des. 25, 1815, and died Des. 30, 1902. He hopt Kooperativ industri wud prov a remedi for poverti. He woz a spelin reformr since 1843 and prepared dis epitaf in sienst spelin in his lif."

CHINA AND THE MARTIN DYNASTY ◼

China's knowledge of the rules of international diplomacy and methods of teaching English to the Chinese can be traced to a Hoosier. He was William Alexander Parson Martin, born at Livonia in 1827 and destined to spend sixty-six years in China, to become an aide to imperial officials and act as their bridge to the advancing technological world.

Although Martin's major influence in China was during the last half of the nineteenth century, its effect can still be glimpsed today in that nation's schools and its use of diplomatic material he translated into Chinese more than 100 years ago.

His arrival in China in 1850 came during a rebellion which was to last until 1865. It was put down with the aid of the British and American governments, which were interested in trade and stability in China. During the unrest, Martin learned to speak two Chinese dialects and to write classical Chinese.

After moving to Beijing and becoming friends with Chinese officials, Martin used his skill to translate into Chinese the bible of diplomacy, Wheaton's *International*

Law. Soon afterward, when China opened the Interpreter's College, Martin became the English teacher and later president. Many graduates became diplomats.

Martin gained the nickname Kuan-hsi, or First among Occidentals, and later gained the rank of governor. However, he always thought of himself as mainly a religious missionary.

In 1894 at the dedication of Kirkwood Hall on the Indiana University Bloomington campus he was cited as an outstanding graduate for his work in international law. He died in 1916, five years after China became a republic.

Today, although China still uses material stemming from Martin's accomplishments, he is among the forgotten in Indiana. A few of his papers can be found at Salem. Foster Quad at I.U., named for John W. Foster, secretary of state under Benjamin Harrison, has a building named for Martin.

■ THE ALMOST PRESIDENT

Dr. John W. Davis of Carlisle may have missed becoming the president of the United States by a single vote. Although there is many a slip 'twixt the convention and the election, the Davis legend goes like this:

Davis and his family arrived in Sullivan County in 1825 by way of Terre Haute from Maryland where he had an unsatisfying medical practice. In politics, however, he prospered because of his magnetic personality and forceful speaking manner, rising through numerous posts from postmaster to the legislature and eventually Congress.

In 1852 he was a delegate to the Democratic Convention in Baltimore, where he was named president of the convention. The nomination battle was deadlocked between Lewis Cass of Michigan, James Buchanan of Pennsylvania, and Stephen Douglas of Illinois. After thirty-five ballots, no man had the necessary majority.

At a compromise session, the names of Franklin Pierce and John W. Davis were introduced. The caucus, deciding which name to present to the convention, chose Pierce by just one vote.

Pierce was nominated and elected. And so the chauvinists of Sullivan County always have felt that their distinguished politician, Dr. Davis, missed the White House by the narrow margin of the caucus balloting.

THE SOULE OF GREELEY ■

Horace Greeley, editor of the *New York Tribune*, didn't create the expression "Go West, young man!"

Despite Greeley's own denial, the saying continues to be credited to him when the real origin rests with John B. L. Soule, young copublisher of Terre Haute's *Wabash Express*.

Soule, urged by Col. Richard Wigginton Thompson, a former Indiana congressman, coined the phrase in an 1854 editorial in which he wrote: "Horace Greeley could never have given a young man better advice than these words, 'Go West, young man.'"

The expression became widely distributed, with the credit going to Greeley despite the fact that he denied authorship in his newspaper on July 13, 1865.

History records little more about what happened to Soule after he wrote his famous words. He had disappeared from Terre Haute by 1858; maybe he went West.

■ MARK OF THE HUNTER

Perhaps thousands of Hoosiers have carved initials in trees, but none possesses the lasting fame of the arboreal autograph in Eagle Creek Park.

Officials claim a beech tree is inscribed with the name of Daniel Boone and his trademark, the outline of a bear paw.

A document posted by park officials relates how the story of the inscription's origin came through Dr. J. Reade. Reade learned of the mark about 1856 from his grandfather, John C. Hume, who settled in the area about 1820. Hume had heard of the tree from David McCurdy, who had settled in what is now Pike Township in Marion County twenty or twenty-five years earlier. That would date the carving to 1800 or before.

Although woodsman Boone was a surveyor for the U.S. government in the Northwest Territory, some say he never came as far north as Indianapolis.

"We figure the tree is 300 years old," says Margaret Mathews, one of those who guides several thousand visitors a year to it.

She estimates that at least 95 percent of the visitors believe that Boone did the carving, now some eight feet off the ground and growing dimmer each year.

■ THIS GUN FOR HIRE

A Hoosier brought the first repeating rifles into warfare and conceived what surely was the nation's first battlefield easy-payment plan.

The gun was an eight-shot carbine invented by Christopher M. Spencer in 1860. When the Union Army ignored the weapon, Spencer went on the road, trying to sell the

150 rifles a day necessary to keep his Boston factory solvent.

He showed the weapon to Gen. William S. Rosecrans and Gen. John T. Wilder of Greensburg, leader of what was to become known as the Lightning Brigade, and artillery Capt. Eli Lilly of Indianapolis, commander of the 18th Indiana Battery.

Rosecrans said no. But Wilder, a determined ex-businessman, wrote his banker for credit and bought 2,000 Spencer rifles.

Soon Wilder's brigade, of men from Illinois and Hoosiers from the 17th Indiana Infantry Regiment, overcame Rebels in the battle at Hoover's Gap in the Cumberland Mountains; the Southern commander believed he was outnumbered because of the Spencer rifles' firepower.

Later, history notes, President Abraham Lincoln fired the rifle and ordered 200,000 of them.

By then perhaps Wilder's men owned their Spencer rifles free and clear. He had allowed his men to use part of each month's $13 pay to repay the cost of the weapons. That was the mundane financial arrangement behind winning a Civil War battle with rifles the soldiers had to buy themselves.

GOING WHOLE HOG ■

Because Judge Jehu T. Elliott of New Castle was quick and witty, Indiana acquired a railroad.

The judge was sent East to obtain financing in the 1850s for a railroad proposed from Logansport through Kokomo, Elwood, Anderson, and New Castle to Richmond. New Yorkers, he found, considered Hoosiers backwoods figures associated with hogs and ague. During a festive occasion, the judge was asked to name Indiana's favorite musical instrument. It was the swinette, he declared, and gave this explanation:

"The swinette is a very simple piece of work. The maker simply constructs a long box and divides it into compartments which decrease in size from left to right. A hog is thrust head foremost into each compartment from the open side and the aperture is closed with a door through which only the tail of the hog protrudes.

"In the largest compartment is a great old boar to represent the deepest bass. The next hog is slightly smaller and has a correspondingly higher squeal. The smallest is a little pig with a high-pitched squeak.

"The performer sits behind the box, places his music before him, and plays the instrument by pulling the tails in much the same way that a piano player strikes the keys. The hogs and pigs respond with the proper notes and produce the most delightful music imaginable."

The Easterners were charmed, gave their blessing and dollars to the railroad, and when the first engine appeared it was named "Swinette." Painted on its side was a picture of Judge Elliott carrying a pig under his arm.

■ THE UNHAPPY WANDERER

Some thought Pollie Barnett was mad. Others suspected she was dangerous; they claimed—without proof—that she burned the barns of people who insulted her. Many testified to her odd lifestyle—sleeping on floors because she disliked beds and carrying her pet cat all day in her arms.

But nobody ever dared to suggest that Pollie, or Poll, as she was called, lacked determination.

For thirty-some years she jogged and walked an estimated 54,000 miles in Greene, Owen, Daviess, Monroe, and Sullivan counties looking for her missing daughter.

Occasionally she would return to her home place to plant a little garden and rest up before renewing her search.

When Poll died, citizens of Linton raised money for a headstone which survives in Fairview Cemetery. Atop it is the sculptured form of the old wanderer's black cat, her constant companion for the last five or six years of her life.

Poll, a Kentuckian whose maiden name was Lay, married George Barnett, a woodchopper, who either died or disappeared. About 1858 she and two daughters moved to old Fairplay, a town south of Worthington.

One day one daughter, Sylvania, fifteen, disappeared. Poll and her other daughter, Angeline, began tramping the countryside seeking the missing girl.

Some say that Poll's daughter was murdered and her body found in the sands of Eel River. Others say the girl's body was hidden in White River near Newberry.

The verse carved on Pollie Barnett's gravestone at Linton refers to her life of roaming in search of her lost daughter. (Photo by the author)

But if that happened, Poll either didn't know it or didn't believe it. She continued to wander, pausing long enough to bury Angeline after she sickened and died.

At last, on February 27, 1900, Poll died too. It was estimated that she had wandered nearly 11,000 days, averaging five miles a day. She was said to have visited 10,000 homes. Her dying words were reported as: "Let my cat go. Let it go to look for Sylvania."

A collection was made for, as the Linton *Democrat* put it, "the old lady whose death is a relief to the worn out, haggard old body." With it the town gave Poll a church funeral and a tombstone that carries this inscription:

> Here Pollie Barnett is at rest
> From deepest grief & toilsome quest.
> Her cat, her only friend,
> Remained with her until life's end.

■ A Man Who . . . And Another Man Who . . . And . . .

In the fall and winter of 1860–61, Indiana had four governors in 105 days, a case of musical chairs in the chief executive's office unmatched before or since.

It began with Ashbel P. Willard of New York who came by way of New Albany and the Indiana General Assembly to the post of governor in 1857. Willard, who had a drinking problem, fell ill, went to Minneapolis to try to regain his health, and died on October 4, 1860. He was the first Hoosier governor to die in office.

His successor was lieutenant governor Abram A. Hammond, a New Englander who had come to Brookville at the age of six. Hammond was to serve the longest—103 days—during this strange period. His term as governor ended with the election of Henry S. Lane as governor and his inauguration on January 14, 1861.

However, Lane had a plan. In those days Indiana's U.S. senators were chosen by the state legislature. Lane had gotten Oliver P. Morton to run with him for lieutenant governor with the promise that Lane would move on to become senator if their fellow Republicans gained control of the legislature. They did, naming Lane senator two days later.

Then Morton took the governor's chair, keeping it through the stormy days of the Civil War and gaining reelection for a second term. So, in one period of 105 days, four men—Willard, Hammond, Lane, and Morton—served as governor of Indiana.

READING, WRITING, AND STAGE FRIGHT ■

The requirement in schools of the 1860s that pupils give weekly recitations from *McGuffey's Fourth Reader* or some other book brought misery to many. But none felt greater fear than one Hoosier boy.

"At sixteen I could seldom repeat the simplest schoolboy speech without breaking down," he said. Sometimes his stuttering and speechlessness caused him to return to his seat to a chorus of derision.

Scheduled to recite the poem about Casabianca, the gallant thirteen-year-old who stood on the burning deck of a warship during a battle off the mouth of the Nile, the schoolboy played hookey to avoid embarrassment.

Once "The Dying Soldier," a poem which moved him to tears, was the class recitation subject. The youth, seeing that his turn to read would come at the climax and knowing this would bring him to tears, fled when the teacher's back was turned. His father asked why he had left school. The boy confessed and received a whipping, an injustice he never forgot—not even when he became Indiana's most famous poet and his name, James Whitcomb Riley, was nationally known.

Strangely enough, the poems he could not read aloud, he could write with skill. And somehow, over the years, he surmounted classroom awkwardness and shyness to become a noted performer, reading his poems and the works of others to audiences throughout the nation.

■ BOGGSTOWN GOES SOUTH

Perhaps it was all a publicity stunt. If so, it worked. To this day Boggstown in Shelby County is known as the only Indiana town to have voted to secede from the Union in the Civil War.

It was a time of political controversy. Shelby County had voted for Stephen Douglas over Abraham Lincoln for president. When rumors started that the South might secede, a meeting was called for February 16, 1861.

Boggstown was seeking a way to improve its image and status. In addition, the community was noted for its spirited debates in an era when debating was a popular recreational activity. So all the ingredients were present to put the town on the map.

With this in mind, Dr. J. W. Smelser, helped by a friend named Fullalove who was visiting from Kentucky, prepared a resolution designed to bring notice to Boggstown and also attract Northerners to the Southern slavery cause.

The best-remembered part of the resolution stated that if the nation were to divide and Boggstown had to make a choice, it would "prefer to be attached to the Southern Confederacy."

Boggstown had Southern sympathizers. In fact, only Dr. William G. McFadden, a new doctor near town, Moses

Gray Tull, and an unidentified third person opposed the resolution. All the others—and attendance was good because the debate had been well publicized—favored seceding.

One speaker characterized the Union side as "hypocritical, cunning, crafty, foxy, blue-bellied Yankees of the New England states." Ben Farmbrough declared that he had done business with both Southerners and Yankees. "Whatever a Kentuckian tells you, you can depend on; he's fair and squar; his word is as good as his bond. As for the blue-bellied Yanks, I've had dealins with them, too; and you've got to watch 'em as well as pray, for prayin' won't do no good; they'll cheat you any chance they git, and make a chance if they don't see one."

Against such rhetoric, McFadden was helpless with his reasoned appeal. "Gentlemen, the people of New England are not all Abolitionists, and they are not all as bad as has been represented," he pleaded to no avail.

When the resolution was approved, Fullalove, as had been planned, carried the news to Kentucky and it was spread widely over the South and West. Partly because of this publicity, not welcomed by everyone, debate meetings in Shelby County waned.

On April 12, when Fort Sumter was fired upon and President Lincoln called for troops, Shelby County, the Boggstown resolution evidently forgotten, raised two full companies of men in two weeks. And, since Boggstown did nothing further when the Union was divided, it is evident that the resolution was eyewash, just as Smelser and Fullalove had in mind.

But as long as the resolution survived in history, Boggstown's odd moment in the limelight remained alive. In 1961 the town rejected a request that the resolution be officially "repealed."

It is true that Boggstown is now a quiet village where a fiery town meeting is as unlikely as a presidential parade.

But its citizens still love to remember the day when their debate caused sparks for miles around, and they have loyally preserved the memory of the secession which never really was.

■ THE LADY ON THE FRONT LINES

During the years he lived in Greensburg, many neighbors came to the home of Civil War veteran John Finnern to hear stories about the war between the states—told by his wife.

Elizabeth Cain Finnern could tell better tales than her husband could because she posed as a Union soldier and fought on the front lines for six months before her masquerade was discovered. Even then she remained with the fighting unit, leaving only to nurse her wounded husband and other sick and wounded. In the years after her death, her Greensburg grave was honored on Memorial Day and Armed Forces Day.

The Finnerns, natives of Germany, lived in Ohio when John became a private in the 81st Ohio Volunteer Infantry in October 1861. Elizabeth volunteered as a nurse-laundress.

Versions differ on how Elizabeth got into the field. One story is that her position as a laundress was abolished by the military, but she was permitted to remain with the troops because of the value of her job and because Gen. John A. Logan had noted the strong bond between the Finnerns.

Another more romantic story is that she was serving in a hospital in Tennessee and, hearing that her husband's unit was surrounded and outnumbered nearby, donned a Union uniform she found in a storeroom. She walked to the battlefield on the slopes of Lookout Mountain, slipped through Confederate lines, and joined her startled husband.

Whichever story is authentic, she did perform like a soldier, carrying a musket when danger threatened, enduring long marches, going without food, and taking part in battles. At times she cared for the wounded, even helping with amputations. It was said that she was at the battles of Corinth, Pocahontas, and Huntsville, Alabama; Harrison, Missouri; and Pulaski, Fort Donaldson, and Chattanooga, Tennessee, among others.

"All I ask is to fight beside John," she said.

When John was wounded in the battle of Arkansas Post, Elizabeth reportedly pushed deep into enemy territory, shooting down the man who had wounded her husband. A fellow soldier in the 81st Ohio, who had followed her, saved Elizabeth from death or capture.

So she was able to follow her husband to the hospital, where he was among some seven hundred wounded. Elizabeth, finding the unit disorganized and improperly directed, took over supervision of scarce supplies. She also was credited with renovating the hospital even while battling an outbreak of scarlet fever.

When John was mustered out of service in September 1864, the couple moved to Indiana. John died in 1905 at Greensburg and the widow who had followed him even into battle became a recluse, jeered at by children but watched over by adults.

Once when she was ill a doctor's wife, duplicating what Elizabeth had done in the army, nursed the former female soldier back to health. She also helped Elizabeth, destitute and in poor health, apply to President Theodore Roosevelt for a pension as a soldier's widow.

But Elizabeth followed her husband in death in July 1907, her pension largely unspent. It was used for a Bedford stone monument to mark the graves of the two battlefield buddies, John and Elizabeth Finnern.

Crawfordsville had only about 2,000 residents when the Civil War began. Yet it provided five generals to the Union, a remarkable contribution for any Hoosier city.

William H. Morgan, John P. Hawkins, Edward R. S. Canby, Mahlon D. Manson, and Lew Wallace all wore general's insignia on their uniforms and called the Montgomery County seat home.

Morgan left Crawfordsville to attend the Naval Academy at Annapolis, served two years in the Navy, and was back home when he became captain of the 10th Indiana Regiment in 1861. He rose to brigadier general, and his service included the Atlanta campaign and the "march to the sea" with Sherman.

Hawkins, a graduate of the military academy at West Point, served in the Vicksburg campaign before being promoted to brigadier general and given command of a black brigade. He served during the war in the Louisiana-Arkansas area.

Canby, a brother-in-law of Hawkins, also was graduated from West Point. At the start of the war Canby was appointed major general of volunteers. He took part in the campaign against Mobile, continued in the Army after the war, and was selected to negotiate peace terms with the Modoc Indians. While talks were in progress Canby and three staff officers were murdered by the renegade leader of the Modocs.

Manson, a druggist, recruited volunteers at Crawfordsville and was commissioned a captain. He earned other promotions, and after the battle of Mill Springs in 1862 he was made a brigadier general of volunteers. Wounds at the battle of Resaca ended his active duty. In 1870 Manson beat his old political rival, Lew Wallace, in the race for congressman. He later was elected state auditor and lieutenant governor and joined the department of internal revenue.

Wallace was not only the most famous of the Crawfordsville generals, he was also the youngest major general in the Union army when he achieved that rank. He had been asked by Gov. Oliver Morton to recruit six regiments from Indiana; Wallace organized thirteen. He was given command of the 11th. When it disbanded because recruitment times had expired and a new 11th was formed, Wallace commanded it in three major battles, including Shiloh, where he was accused of arriving late—a blunder some historians say was not Wallace's fault.

Wallace later was governor of the New Mexico Territory, was minister to Turkey, and became famous as an author after the publication of his book, *Ben Hur.*

THE GAT WITH A MISSION ■

Long before the mid-twentieth century Cold War, a Hoosier physician developed the idea of deterrence as a barrier to war. But a look at the sophisticated, mass-killing weapons of today shows that Richard Jordan Gatling's theory has so far not proven correct.

A talented inventor as well as a doctor, Gatling had already developed a cottonseed planter, a rice and wheat driller, a steam plow, and a hemp carding machine. He got the idea as he was sitting in his Indianapolis office, watching men march off to the Civil War: Why not devise a weapon which would be so decisive in battle that no foe would dare attack the side that had it?

"I thought if war was made more terrible, it would have a tendency to keep peace among nations," Gatling later explained, "and such is getting to be the case. . . . This country pays $130 million in pensions annually. Half of that expended on Gatling guns would keep the peace of the world."

This gun, put together in six weeks by machinist Otis Frink from Gatling's drawings, put six rotating rifle barrels together (later it was made with ten barrels). With one man cranking the barrels and another doing the sighting, the gun could fire bullets from a hopper with great speed. In a demonstration near White River in Indianapolis the new gun cranked off two pounds of lead bullets in thirty seconds. Later, the gun was remodeled to fire 200 shots a minute, and by 1898, one electrically powered from a battery was capable of 3,000 rounds a minute.

Purchasers and peace did not rush to Gatling's doorstep. Indiana governor Oliver P. Morton urged adoption of the gun to P. H. Watson, assistant secretary of war. But Gen. James Wolfe Ripley, chief of ordnance and a believer in traditional weapons, hindered a test.

Only twelve guns were built during the Civil War by a firm at Cincinnati. Gen. Benjamin F. Butler bought two of the guns, the only models to be used during the war. They helped him hold a bridge head.

Gatling had some success elsewhere. Napoleon III bought some guns in Paris. The weapon was used during the Philippine insurrection, against Spanish cavalry in Cuba, in the Franco-Prussian War. The British used it throughout their empire and the Gatling gun barked during the Boxer Rebellion. One was mounted on a vehicle to create the first armored car. The Gatling was manufactured by Cooper's Firearms Manufactory at Philadelphia, Colt Armory at Hartford, Connecticut, and by licensees in Russia, Austria, Turkey, and England. Gen. George Custer had four Gatling guns under his command when he reached the Little Big Horn, but he had left all four behind.

Gatling, not averse to making money while ending war, saw meager profit from the gun. Continual changes in caliber from country to country required costly retooling. But he never abandoned his theory: ". . . Have one man do the work of a hundred—and let the other ninety-nine stay home."

His weapon, adopted by the U.S. Army in 1866, was declared obsolete in 1911. It has been followed by numerous rapid-fire guns. In 1956 General Electric unveiled a six-barrel aerial cannon called the Vulcan, capable of firing 7,000 rounds a minute. Gatling's original patents were closely studied in development of the Vulcan, the engineers said.

In more than a century since Gatling got his patent on November 4, 1862, the world appears to have come no closer to his elusive dream—a weapon fearsome enough to end war.

COWED AT VERNON ■

One of those embarrassing moments in the Civil War occurred at Vernon when the home guard and militia faced Morgan's Raiders in 1863. Morgan called for the town to surrender, but the commander refused; he asked for time to evacuate the noncombatants.

Morgan agreed, and while the town was making preparations he set up a screen of skirmishers and moved most of his force southeastward toward Dupont. By the time darkness fell, the Vernon defenders, unaware of Morgan's departure, were certain an attack was pending.

When great splashing was heard from Finney's Ford, a stream at the southeastern edge of town, the panicky home guard in that sector took to their heels. Many fell from a twenty-foot embankment in the scramble to escape what they thought were Morgan's seasoned troops. More men were hurt in the retreat than were wounded in Indiana by Morgan's firepower.

Too late did Vernon's defenders learn that the noise

they heard had been livestock being driven across the ford to reach the safety of the town; the Battle of Finney's Ford was over as quickly as it had begun.

■ DESERTION AND DISGRACE

The first and only Union soldier executed in the West in the Civil War was a private from Clay County, killed by a firing squad at Camp Morton in Indianapolis. He was charged with desertion; some historians contend his execution was based on flimsy evidence and carried out deviously to gain promotion for some of the officers involved.

Robert Gay joined Company D, 71st Indiana Regiment in August 1862. He had been a school teacher in Clay County. His poor health and frail condition made him unfit for service, but he was kept in the unit until the battle of Richmond, Kentucky, when he and others in the regiment were captured.

Most of the others were paroled by the Confederacy, but Gay swore allegiance to the South to obtain medical treatment and permission to return home to Ohio. It was claimed by some that he did not understand the seriousness of his action. When he was later arrested, a paper showing his oath to the South was found in the cuff of his trousers.

Gay was executed March 27, 1863, at Burnside barracks, Camp Morton. Noted one historical writer: "His mistake . . . did not justify the military in selecting him, as one of thousands more guilty than he was, just because he had no family dependent on him, or relatives, or friends to appeal to President Lincoln for pardon."

It is claimed that in Indiana alone there were 2,000 deserters in December 1862. Not one of them was executed.

In his Civil War unit, A. B. Crampton was somewhat unusual because he was the first Hoosier sworn into it—Company A of the 48th Indiana Infantry—and lived to be its last surviving member. But his strangest Civil War experience was publishing an edition of the newspaper at Vicksburg, Mississippi, deep in Southern territory.

The July 4, 1863, issue was unusual not only in that it provided Crampton with an opportunity to answer a Southern editor's dig at the Yankees, but also because it was printed on wallpaper.

The siege of Vicksburg ended July 4. A few days earlier, Gen. U. S. Grant, knowing he would need printing facilities as soon as he entered the city, called for volunteers. Crampton, a color sergeant in his unit, was appointed foreman of a trio who applied for the task.

At the *Vicksburg Citizen* they found the July 2 issue ready to be printed on the blank side of wallpaper since supplies of all other paper had long since been exhausted in the city. The Southern editor had written: "The great Ulysses—the Yankee generalissimo, surnamed Grant—has expressed his intention of dining in Vicksburg on Saturday next and celebrating the Fourth of July by a grand dinner and so forth. When asked if he would invite Gen. Jo Jackson to join, he said, 'No, for fear there would be a row at the table.' Ulysses must get into the city before he dines in it. The way to cook a rabbit is first to catch the rabbit."

Crampton thought an updating was necessary. He rearranged the article to leave room for his reply: "Two days bring about great changes. The banner of the Union floats over Vicksburg. Gen. Grant has 'caught the rabbit,' he has dined in Vicksburg and did bring his dinner with him. The *Citizen* lives to see it. For the last time it appears on wall paper. No more will we eulogize the luxury of mule meat and fricasseed kitten—urge Southern warriors to such diet nevermore. This is the last 'wall paper' edition and is, excepting this note, from the types as we found them. It will be valuable hereafter as a souvenir."

Crampton was right. Regular paper arrived the next day, and he used it and the newspaper's equipment to publish dispatches.

A veteran of newspaper work for sixty years both before and after the Civil War, Crampton was living in Indianapolis on March 5, 1933, when he celebrated his ninetieth birthday by showing off his copy of the Vicksburg wallpaper edition.

■ HOOSIERS AWEIGH

If you think Indiana never had a Navy, you are forgetting the Civil War battle won with a single shot from a Hoosier ship. It is known as the Battle of Blue River Island.

In 1863, shortly before the famed Morgan raid into Indiana, Thomas W. Hines of Bowling Green, Kentucky, led a cavalry company across the Ohio River into Perry County. The men fanned out, looking for horses.

Whenever questioned, the men said they were with the Home Guard; there were a lot of men moving about in uniform and the Home Guard was very loosely organized. But increased scrutiny led the Confederates to realize they were under suspicion. They fled Marengo, followed by Martin Stewart and John Vanmeter. These two Hoosier Paul Reveres bypassed the Confederates and aroused Paoli to prepare for the oncoming enemy troops; Hines and his men turned to the Ohio.

Near what is now the Harrison-Crawford State Forest, they were attacked by Home Guard units and forced into the water, wading to Blue River Island. Technically they were on Kentucky soil, but they also were trapped—attackers on one side, the deep main channel on the other.

Shots were exchanged. When a towboat appeared, Hines called it to the island.

Before Hines's army could embark, the *Izetta* hove into view from Leavenworth. Wash Lyons, captain of this small steamboat, signaled the towboat to move away, which it did. Then he fired a shot at the Confederates from his six-pound cannon.

The Southerners, who had started a last-ditch swim for the distant river bank, floundered back onto the island and gave up.

Start the Presses ■

The greenback, the form of currency which gets its name from its color, has been with us for more than 125 years in varying forms. And counterfeiting of greenbacks has been with us just as long.

The first counterfeiting of those bills occurred in Indianapolis. And the counterfeiter got away with it—after a daring escape.

Greenbacks came into existence in 1862. By the next spring federal agents in Washington, D.C., were asked to help Indianapolis policemen find the source of phony bills which were flooding the city.

The bills were the work of Thomas Peter McCartney and the Johnson family of Lawrence, just outside Indianapolis. The Johnsons were noted criminals of pre–Civil War America and McCartney was one of their recruits. The Johnsons—grandfathers, father, sons, mothers, and daughters—were crack passers of fake bank notes, drafts, and currency. William Johnson, the most gifted engraver of the clan, taught the art to McCartney.

Whereas the Johnsons specialized in passing fake $1

bills issued by area banks, McCartney, more ambitious, starting passing $10s. He passed his first phony $10 in a small grocery store near Union Station just before the Civil War.

Emboldened by success, the Johnsons and McCartney started counterfeiting green backs as soon as they appeared. The Johnsons produced the bills in Lawrence and they were circulated through McCartney' downtown Indianapolis business enterprises; he entered into real estate deals in the booming economy as a means of laundering the money.

But then the Johnsons decided to deal McCartney out. How he learned of their scheme is not known, but he went to Lawrence, stole the counterfeiting plates, had them electrotyped, and returned the originals without arousing the Johnsons' suspicions. McCartney had matched betrayal with betrayal. With two sets of plates operating, the increase in phony money in Indianapolis alerted authorities.

Faced with disastrous inflation if the counterfeiting went unchecked, Indianapolis welcomed a team of federal agents led by Maj. William P. Wood, superintendent of the Old Capitol Prison in Washington, a man described as "vindictive, cunning and ambitious."

Checking anybody who passed a bogus greenback (many citizens had come into possession of the bills through innocent transactions), the government team followed a careless confederate to the Johnsons and one of them, seeking a deal, implicated McCartney. McCartney was seized, chained, and whisked aboard a Washington-bound train.

But the man who dared to be a counterfeiter also had courage enough to escape, leaping from a train going thirty-five miles an hour. Although injured, he found his way to friends and returned to Indianapolis. Because authorities had failed to search his quarters, he regained the plates and, after eluding a manhunt, resumed passing bogus bills in Indianapolis and various parts of the Midwest.

When McCartney died on October 21, 1890, at the age of sixty-six, it was estimated that he had made more than fifty sets of plates and circulated more than $1 million in bogus bills. But his first venture was in Indianapolis, making Indiana the birthplace of the phony greenback.

THE ASSASSINATION ASSEMBLAGE ■

On the day Abraham Lincoln was shot, his last caller was a Hoosier who declined an invitation to accompany the president to the theater. Had he accepted, he would have been seated with Lincoln when he was assassinated.

As it was, three Hoosiers did see the assassination, and two of them were among the first to reach the fallen president. The other Hoosier "donated" an Indiana flag for use in Ford's Theater for a renowned photograph of the assassination site.

Two Hoosiers also were with Lincoln when he died the morning after the shooting.

Lincoln's last caller was Schuyler Colfax, congressman from Indiana, speaker of the House of Representatives, and a close friend of Lincoln's. Colfax was preparing to travel west to promote railroad development. Lincoln, much interested in Colfax's trip, spoke to the South Bend Republican on April 14, 1865, and invited Colfax to come with him to see *Our American Cousin*. Colfax declined because of another appointment and because he needed to prepare for his trip. He reported later his hand was grasped by Lincoln, who said, "Pleasant journey to you, good-bye."

"And that was his last good-bye on earth," Colfax declared.

Although Colfax wasn't in Ford's Theater that evening, John S. Duncan, Samuel E. Tillford, and W. H. DeMotte were. Tillford, a former employee of the *Indianapolis Journal* and now an infantryman, was in Washington on army business. With him in the theater was Duncan, an Indianapolis criminal lawyer. The two noticed John Wilkes Booth, the well-known actor, moving about the theater and, like many in the audience, thought the shots were part of the play. Tillford reported that he and Duncan were among the first to rush to Lincoln's balcony. "Two or three others beat us there," he declared.

Directly across from Lincoln's balcony sat W. H. De-Motte of Indianapolis, later a teacher at the state school for the blind. DeMotte was then stationed at the Indiana state military office in Washington, near Ford's Theater.

Next day a photographer for *Harper's Weekly* showed up at DeMotte's office asking to borrow an Indiana flag. Numerous flags had been used as decorations round Lincoln's box, but the Indiana flag had been torn down. DeMotte provided a flag, and the photographer put it in place before recording the scene of the crime. The next day the theater was closed and placed under federal control. When DeMotte sought his flag, officials of the provost marshal's office said they were unaware of its existence. "So the state of Indiana lost a nice flag, but has the honor of contributing to the makeup of the first picture of the scene published by *Harper's Weekly*," DeMotte said later.

When Colfax heard of the shooting, he went to the house where Lincoln had been carried and was there when the president died. Also present was Hugh McCullough of Fort Wayne, a key figure in Indiana banking and Lincoln's secretary of the treasury. He had been the first U.S. comptroller of the currency.

McCullough reported later on the silence of the bedroom scene. Only when Mrs. Lincoln came in were sounds of grief evident as she wept. After she left, quiet again descended. "It continued unbroken until seven o'clock in the morning when the death shade came over [Lincoln's] face," McCullough reported.

Colfax became vice-president under Grant. Tainted by a railroad construction scandal, Colfax did not run for reelection. He retired from public life in 1872, and often lectured on his favorite topic, "My Friend, Abraham Lincoln."

McCullough continued to serve as secretary of the treasury under President Andrew Johnson, retiring in 1869. After a time in banking in London, McCullough was persuaded by President Chester A. Arthur to return to the post, replacing Walter Q. Gresham of Indiana, who had resigned. Serving to the end of Arthur's term, McCullough retired at the age of seventy-six and died ten years later.

COURTHOUSE TREE-TOP TALL ■

History suggests M. J. Willey is the tourism hero of Greensburg. He is the man often credited with sighting the first tree growing from the Decatur County courthouse tower, a whimsy of nature which has made Greensburg internationally known.

The date of the first tree probably was 1865 or 1866. Certainly early in the 1870s the first sprig was spotted on the northwest corner of the courthouse tower, 110 feet above the ground. As it grew, so did its popularity. In 1875 another tree appeared and county officials, who had feared the growth might damage the stone-slab roof, bowed to the inevitable. Woodsmen were ordered to spare the tree. It finally was cut down in 1919 after it had grown twelve feet tall with a trunk four inches in diameter.

But other trees took its place. By 1927 the ninth had appeared. In 1932 A. H. Winders, a steeplejack from

The courthouse tower at Greensburg is known worldwide because of the tree growing on its roof. (Photo by the author)

Redkey, put six steel bands in place to gird the tower roof against the force of the roots.

Tree No. 10 was removed in 1950 and tree No. 11 was discovered in 1953. One tree started growing inside the tower and had to be redirected out through a crevice. The twelfth tree, which survives today, sprouted in 1958, the same year that Old No. 9, by then thirty-one years old, was removed; its fifteen-inch-wide trunk was considered too much weight for the roof to withstand.

Along with the mystery of where the trees originated and why they persisted growing was the question of the species. Officials of the Smithsonian Institution determined that the trees are large tooth aspen, dismissing guesses that they might have been linden or silver poplars.

Each year a steeplejack trims the growth on the tower and inspects it for damage. But after 130 years Greensburg is committed to preserving the trees that have brought visitors from every state in the Union, given rise to newspaper and magazine stories all over the world, been used as the name for athletic teams, and inspired songs and poems.

One, by Smiley Fowler, a long-time Indiana newspaper columnist, seems to tell it well:

> On the roof of our tower, two trees
> Seem to thrive in the dust laden breeze,
>   But when the storm blows,
>   The Lord only knows,
> How they cling with such nonchalant ease.

THE GIRL WHO WASN'T THERE ∎

Mary Roff, born in Warren County, died when she was nineteen years old. But thirteen years later, in a well-documented case of parapsychology, she "came back" in the body of another female to spend fifteen weeks with her astonished parents. A girl named Lurancy Vennum seemed to literally become Mary Roff, according to numerous witnesses. She lived with Mary's parents, conversed with them about bygone happenings, identified pictures and documents from the past, and described relatives. Then "Mary Roff" declared that it was time to leave and Lurancy Vennum "returned," feeling that she had been asleep for a long time.

Mary Roff was born October 8, 1846, to Mr. and Mrs. Asa Roff in Warren County. When she was thirteen her parents moved to Watseka, Illinois. There Mary began to have seizures similar to those of an epileptic. She slashed her wrists. Saved from suicide, she became violent for a time, then calmed. On July 5, 1865, she died during a visit to friends at Peoria. The coroner blamed brain convulsions for the death.

Lurancy Vennum had been born fifteen months before

Mary died to Mr. and Mrs. Thomas Vennum in Iowa. In 1871, six years after Mary's death, the Vennums moved to Watseka. Mary and Lurancy had never met.

Lurancy began seeing images at night in her room, began to enter states where she stiffened, sometimes bending so far backward that her head and feet touched. The Roffs, hearing of the trances, were reminded of their dead daughter, and they contacted the Vennums.

Learning that an asylum had been suggested for Lurancy, the Roffs suggested Dr. E. Winchester Stevens of Janesville, Wisconsin, be consulted. Dr. Stevens arrived on January 31, 1878.

A short time later Lurancy became "possessed" by Mary Roff, who replaced a much angrier "person" who had spoken through Lurancy. Mary, sweet and polite, wanted to go home to her family. The Roffs hesitated, doubtful, thinking the aberration would go away. It didn't. On February 11, 1878, Lurancy Vennum went to live with the reluctant and skeptical Roffs as the spirit of their daughter Mary.

Newspapers were fascinated with the story. Dr. Stevens, who observed the remarkable personality transfer, wrote a book about it, *The Watseka Wonder*, although he was unable to ascertain if Lurancy actually had become Mary and, if so, what had happened to Lurancy in the meantime.

The Vennum girl had no answers either when she "came back" on May 21, 1878. Dr. Stevens found that the revived Lurancy was in good health mentally and physically and that when she wrote, it was in her hand and not in that of Mary Roff. Comparisons of the writing of Lurancy as herself and as Mary Roff bore no resemblance to each other, the doctor reported.

Lurancy Vennum, who became Mrs. George Binning, lived well into her seventies, declining in later years to discuss the incident which had for a time propelled her into the baffling role of the Watseka wonder.

THE CIRCUS'S GREATEST COUP ■

Barnum could have exhibited William Cameron Coup. He was that much of a wonder.

The Hoosier Coup was the general behind many of the developments which ushered in the golden age of the circus; he created a spectacular show which for the first time used the full potential of rail transportation.

Coup's idea of traveling by rail enabled the show to bypass small towns and play the more profitable large cities. He originated the idea of "piggyback" cars, which could be loaded without waste space and hoisted onto regular railroad flatcars. Coup introduced the center pole for the big top, perfected posters and billboards as advertising avenues, and persuaded railroads to run one-day and half-fare excursions to bring customers to the circus.

Adventure entered Coup's blood early. Born at Mount Pleasant, Indiana, in 1837, the son of the innkeeper, he left home to become a traveling printer. In 1850 he joined a small circus, fell in love with the gypsy life, and worked several shows before joining with Don Costello, a former clown, in Costello's Floating Carnival and Grand Menagerie.

In 1870 Phineas T. Barnum, who had gained fame for his museums and stage tours, was restive in retirement in Bridgeport, Connecticut. Coup obtained his financial backing and the use of his name for the Barnum-Coup-Costello Circus, "The Great Enterprise."

It opened April 10, 1871, in Brooklyn under three acres of canvas with a herd of 600 horses to take it on the road. As the result of Coup's concept, the circus traveled in the spring of 1872 in sixty-one cars rented from the Pennsylvania Railroad. The show grossed $1 million in six months. The only other show to have used railroads had gone broke.

Soon Coup designed his own piggyback cars and made other improvements. In 1874 the show was larger than any ever seen before, leasing an entire block on what later was the site of Madison Square Garden. P. T. Barnum's Great Roman Hippodrome was 200 feet wide and 426 feet long. It traveled in 100 railroad cars, all painted garishly to advertise the circus.

When Barnum leased the use of his name to a small, cheap wagon show in 1875, the angry Coup sold out his interest. He opened a successful aquarium on Broadway, parted with his partner in a disagreement over Sunday shows, opened his own circus, New United Monsters Shows, in 1879, but lost it in a railroad wreck when the equipment burned. Coup retired to Florida and died in 1895.

Years later his ideas still lived when Ringling Brothers and Barnum and Bailey Combined Shows, "The Greatest Show on Earth," became the only surviving circus in the nation still traveling on the rails.

■ BURNING DESIRE TO DIE

They may not remember James A. Moon around Lafayette anymore, but he was the farmer who committed suicide with a candle.

Moon, thirty-seven, who lived nine miles west of Lafayette, checked into Room 41 on the third floor of the Lahr Hotel in Lafayette on June 10, 1876. After getting a shave, chatting with old Civil War army comrades around town, and having a porter carry a heavy trunk to his room, Moon retired about 9:00 P.M., never to be seen alive again.

The guillotine with which Moon killed himself was described by Dr. W. W. Vinnedge, Tippecanoe County coroner. A framework was fastened to the floor with hinges. A broadax on the end of a seven-foot lever was elevated and held aloft by a double cord fastened to a bracket which was attached to the woodwork at the side of a window in the room. A lighted candle was placed between the twin cords.

Then Moon fastened himself to the floor with straps and buckles and put his head inside a soap box placed on its side. The soap box contained cotton saturated with chloroform to put Moon in a stupor so that he couldn't halt the events he had put in motion or feel any pain.

When the candle burned down to the proper point, the flame ignited the cords; when they burned in two, the broadax fell, severing Moon's head from his body.

The gadget was complicated but efficient.

Moon, a self-taught blacksmith always interested in mechanics, had inscribed his guillotine lever with the words, "Kari Kan," "Patent Applied For," and "For Sale or To Let."

ATTRACTIVE WATER ■

People for miles around were drawn to Jim Bailey's well near Plymouth.

And it was magnetic to more than people. Knives, shears, scissors, hooks, and small bars of steel became magnetized when placed in the water. From two feet away the water could totally control a compass needle.

Its output, an estimated 500 gallons a minute, 720,000 gallons a day, was enough in 1876 to supply a city of 50,000 inhabitants. It was, by all estimates, the largest magnetized well ever drilled in Indiana.

But it was not what Bailey had wanted. His firm had been trying to open a seam to operate a mill wheel by underground currents. Instead they got the gusher whose cold flow sparkled with the tints of the rainbow.

What became of the well during more than 100 years is unknown. And there is no telling how many Hoosiers bathed in its flow believing—as many did then—that magnetism would restore health, treat rheumatism and dyspepsia, and make the halt walk.

Whether or not that was true, it is certain that hundreds were lured as if magnetized to the flowing well of Plymouth.

■ THE ONE AND ONLY CURVE-BALL PITCHER

Hoosiers first learned that a baseball could be pitched in a curve one day in 1877, with Eddie (The One and Only) Nolan tossing the horsehide and David Starr Jordan, later to be president of Stanford University and Indiana University, swearing that it couldn't be done.

Nolan had come to Indianapolis from sandlot fame at St. Louis to pitch for the Indianapolis entry in the International League. With him came barehand catcher Frank (Silver) Flint. W. B. Petit's team had won the pennant in 1876 and intended to repeat—with the help of Nolan and Flint.

Nolan was well on his way to getting the job done that summer, mowing down batters and prompting rumors that he could throw a curve, something new in baseball. The pitcher admitted that he could curve the ball; he called it his in-shoot.

"That is a feat," said Jordan, then a science teacher at Butler University, "that is incapable of demonstration."

Maybe so, said Nolan. But the boys at Firehouse No. 7 decided to prove Nolan pitched a curve. They were behind him; most of the Indianapolis scientific community supported Jordan.

Paper was stretched between two sets of posts ten feet apart, placed another ten feet from a brick wall. The idea was for Nolan to toss a ball covered with chalk. Measurements of holes created in the paper and chalk left on the brick wall should show whether or not the baseball curved. It did. Dr. Jordan said he wouldn't have believed it if he hadn't seen it.

Pretty soon a lot of pitchers caught on and today we know that a baseball can be curved from ten to seventeen inches for the same reason that an airplane flies—spin and speed creating high and low areas of pressure.

Uneasy Rests the Head of State ■

President William Henry Harrison feared that after his death his body might be stolen from the grave. But his body rested safe in North Bend Cemetery near Cincinnati, where it was interred in 1841.

It was the body of Harrison's son which was stolen from that same graveyard thirty-seven years later.

William Henry Harrison, governor of the Indiana Territory and hero of the Battle of Tippecanoe, died after only a month in the White House. When his body was shipped to North Bend, circumstantial evidence substantiated the rumor that he feared grave robbing, a fairly common occurrence in those days.

Five coffins were used. The president's body was placed in a lead coffin of double thickness. Around that was a mahogany coffin an inch thick, covered with silk velvet. Next was a coffin of zinc, encased by a coffin of walnut, which had been made water tight. The outside, fifth coffin was panelled oak, according to documents filed by John Williams, a Washington funeral director who reported on the president's burial arrangements to a congressional committee.

Harrison's son, John Scott Harrison, died on May 25, 1878. When he was buried in North Bend cemetery, evidence that a nearby grave had been disturbed caused the family to guard against bodysnatchers. They ordered John Harrison's coffin encased in a brick wall covered by a heavy stone set in concrete. But five days later, while looking for the stolen body of a friend, the Harrison family was dismayed to discover that John Harrison's body had indeed been stolen.

Benjamin Harrison, then an Indianapolis attorney and later to be U.S. president, was notified of the theft of his father's corpse. He joined in an immediate investigation of the Ohio Medical College at Cincinnati, where the body had been found. John Harrison's body had been concealed in a chute which connected upper and lower floors of the building. Benjamin Harrison charged that school officials knew of the grave robbing and the identity of the ghouls, an accusation proven a few days later when an article of clothing which had been on John Harrison's body was found in the school attic.

A notorious bodysnatcher and the school's janitor were indicted in the case. Rumors were that charges were dropped after Harrison's body was returned to the family for reburial.

It is believed by some that Benjamin Harrison's participation in the case and his political stature helped speed passage of laws which established legal means for medical schools to obtain cadavers.

Allan Pinkerton, head of the famed detective agency, which had aided the investigation, issued a bill for $101.35 for helping find the stolen body of the son and father of U.S. presidents.

Who was the tallest Hoosier of all times?

A good candidate has to be the man buried in prehistory days near Brewersville in Jennings County. Unearthed in 1879, the intact skeleton showed him to have been nine feet, eight inches tall. The remains were found in a mound, three to five feet high and seventy-one feet in diameter.

Skeletons were first found there in 1865 when a farmer named Robison was digging to get stones for a spring house. He unearthed the remains of a child. The excitement it caused was remembered by the farmer's son, George M. Robison, who later retold it.

The tall skeleton was found during explorations by the state geologist, who brought witnesses from Cincinnati and New York, accompanied by Dr. Charles Green of North Vernon. Around the neck of the skeleton was a necklace of mica. An image of burned clay embedded with pieces of flint rock stood at the skeleton's feet.

Farmer Robison related that the scientists said the skeleton was that of a member of a white race which predated the redmen in Indiana. No sign of pottery or metal working was found. "We know not whence they came or where they went," the investigators reportedly said.

In later years four others from that area recalled the incident. Robison reportedly kept the burned clay image and some of the bones, which survived for many years in a basket at the Kellar Mill along Sand Creek about a mile from the mound. Robison's grandson, Kenneth Kellar, said the artifacts were lost in the 1937 flood.

Hoaxes come and go, but Indiana has one phony story that survived a hundred years to be revived in the space age.

The bizarre tale of Leonidas Grover of Fountain County came back to life in the late 1970s when debris from outer space satellites began coming back to earth. The prospect of being struck by a hunk of Skylab was alarming, but space authorities assured the public that no deaths had ever been caused by meteors and meteorites—or anything else identifiable as falling from outer space.

Not so, cried readers who remembered the meteor story. One of them, David C. Smith of Indianapolis, notified *Omni,* a slick science-oriented magazine, about the startling case of Grover, and the Hoosier hoax became current again.

According to the story in the Indianapolis *Journal* on January 16, 1879, poor Grover went to sleep in his rural bed while his daughter and her husband were away for the evening. Suddenly a twenty-pound meteor tore through the roof of the house, passed through Grover's body and the bed like a cannon ball, and buried itself five feet deep in the cellar. His daughter and her mate, not detecting anything wrong, retired when they arrived home, so Grover's mutilated body was not discovered until the next morning.

This yarn, investigation later showed, was "planted" on the telegraph news desk of the *Journal* by someone whose identity was never learned. Other newspapers picked up the strange item. Grover's fate became widely publicized.

Among readers was Edward T. Cox, then the state geologist. He thought the meteor should be recovered and sent his neighbor, Maj. John J. Palmer, to Covington to get the killer stone. Palmer quickly discovered there was no Leonidas Grover, no penetrated bed, no meteor. But when his gaze fell on an oblong stone and he reflected on how Cox had sent him on a wild-goose chase, he plotted a hoax of his own.

After painting the stone with red ink and heating it in a fire, Palmer headed back to Indianapolis, seeking his revenge on Cox and also on colleagues of a literary society of which they both were members.

When salesmen on the train, who had heard about Palmer's trip, chided him about the fool's errand, he brought out the "meteor" as proof. They bought the story. There was no turning back. Palmer, adding details as he went along, helped spread the remarkable meteor mishap story. More newspaper reports resulted.

Sightseers became so numerous that Palmer gladly accepted an offer by Joe Perry to exhibit the meteor in his drugstore in downtown Indianapolis.

Of course, when the newspapers learned the truth, they retracted the story. But too many bits about the phony demise of Leonidas Grover had slipped into print. The *Illustrated Police News,* a lurid weekly, had used the story. And Alexander Winchell, a noted geologist, used it in one of his scientific works.

In 1880, the year after the hoax, John Collett, who succeeded Cox as state geologist, wrote a letter to Major Palmer asking him to dig up his famous meteor. People were driving Collett crazy to see the fatal aerolite and Collett, for one, thought it should be in the state museum.

In the museum it evidently stayed, after Palmer retrieved it from the cellar of Perry's drug store. But it disappeared some time after Collett left office.

But the proof that the spirit of the rock and its fictitious victim lingers for easy resurrection is the fact that a century later space officials were sent chasing after the tale. They found John Selch, who operates the newspaper section of the Indiana State Library. His research and recollection of historic oddities quickly proved the story false, thus rendering modern-day earthmen safe again from outer space debris.

■ THE DOME THAT DAUNTS SCIENCE

What has been described as the most spectacular natural phenomenon in Indiana is a hole in the ground near Kentland.

Some tremendous force fractured rocks usually found 1,800 feet below the earth's surface on a horizontal plane and turned them so they now stand vertically. Some are almost at the soil's surface.

The site, in the midst of level, placid farmland, has been an oddity since it was found in the 1880s. Its origin has remained an enigma.

Some contend that only a giant meteorite could have caused the condition. Others believe that a sudden, explosive escape of underground gases could have created the Kentland Dome, as it is called.

Since scientists can make only educated guesses, the Kentland Dome remains one of Indiana's greatest geological mysteries.

■ FROM A RELIABLE SOURCE . . .

William Blodgett, a young reporter for the Anderson *Review-Democrat* in the 1880s, is the only Indiana newspaperman known to have covered a murder before it happened.

A salesman visiting the nearby town of Alexandria was stabbed by a farmer; the salesman won an indictment against his assailant. But friends of the farmer kept helping him get continuances, requiring the salesman to make repeated trips between Anderson and Cleveland, Ohio, his headquarters. At the third court hearing, the salesman told Blodgett that he was going to shoot the farmer if he won another continuance.

Unable to dissuade the salesman, Blodgett rushed to the paper, wrote two stories—one saying the farmer had been wounded and one saying he had been killed—and told the printer to wait for his signal.

When Blodgett witnessed the farmer being shot outside the courthouse, he signaled the printer to put the "murder" version in the edition.

It was slightly premature; the farmer didn't die until two editions later.

The Benefactor of Books ■

In 1880 the Library of Congress had grown to a public reference institution for the entire nation, but it lacked a home. Now a Hoosier rose to plead for one.

He was Daniel W. Voorhees, who grew up in Covington, earned a reputation for great jury speeches and forensic ability, opposed Abraham Lincoln's policies while avoiding any taint of treason, a man who was to be known as the father of the Congressional Library.

Voorhees had entered Congress in 1860. In 1877 he was appointed to the Senate to fill the chair left by the death of Oliver P. Morton, and in 1879 Voorhees won another term.

"To neglect the proper care of such a source of information and of light, or to leave it in jeopardy an hour longer than is now possible appears little less than a crime against civilization and progress," Voorhees told the Senate in May 1880. "We all eagerly turn to it in order to renew our strength for the conflicts of life. Those who drink most deeply at its spring are the strongest and most enduring."

After his speech, the Senate named him chairman of the joint select committee to construct the library, a $5.5 million building complete in 1897.

But he did not live to see the dream fulfilled. As they began moving in the books, Voorhees died. He was buried in Terre Haute's Highland Lawn Cemetery, never to know how well his pet project was to serve the nation.

His contribution was later memorialized on a tablet in the library, provided by the Business and Professional Women's Club of Covington, which quoted from his speech that gave the library its start: "Let us give the national library our love and our care. Nothing can surpass it in importance."

■ ALL SHIPS ABOARD

If a Lawrenceburg engineering genius had been heeded, ships would have had a route from the Atlantic to the Pacific Ocean years before the Panama Canal was finished; they would have made the trip by rail.

James B. Eads, known for the St. Louis bridge across the Mississippi River which many engineers said couldn't be built, made his proposal about 1880. He planned a six-track railway to carry ships 143 miles across the Isthmus of Tehuantepec in Mexico. A train would run on four of the tracks. Two tracks would carry tenders with coal and water. Every ship would be supported by 1,200 wheels, each stabilized by strong steel springs.

For seven years Eads fought for Congressional approval and funds for his plan, without success. He died with his idea bottled up in the House of Representatives.

It was thirty-five years after the Eads idea that the

first ships passed through the Panama Canal locks, miles from the site he had proposed and light years from the method he had envisioned.

NEED A BODY CRY ■

John Brown's body may have moldered in his grave, but the body of his son ended up hanging in an Indiana closet.

Brown and his son, Watson, both were killed at Harpers Ferry in October 1859, in a prelude to the Civil War.

Watson Brown's body was preserved, put in a barrel, and sent to a medical school at Winchester, Virginia. When Dr. Jarvis Johnson of the 27th Regiment of Indiana Volunteers arrived at Winchester with occupation troops in 1862, he took possession of the medical college. Soon he learned that he also possessed Watson Brown's body and that Southerners wanted it. Johnson refused to turn over the body, saying it symbolized the battle against slavery.

What happened next was described by Johnson in an affidavit in 1882. "I, afterward, in the summer of 1862, shipped the body by express via Franklin, Indiana, that point being the nearest express office to my own home, then Morgantown, Indiana, and the said specimen has been in my possession and under my control ever since," Johnson swore. "And I have no doubt whatever but that it is the son of the heroic John Brown."

When Johnson and his family moved to Martinsville, the body, by then reduced to a skeleton, was kept in a second-floor closet on a sun porch.

After Johnson learned in 1882 of a monument to the memory of John Brown and read that Mrs. Brown knew nothing of what happened to the bodies of two of her sons, he notified her that he had the skeleton of Watson Brown.

John Brown, Jr., traveled to Martinsville and, with Dr. Johnson and the state geologist, John Collett, authenticated the identity of the skeleton. It was taken to North Elba, New York, and placed in the family burial ground—the end of one of the most bizarre journeys of any casualty of the Civil War.

■ INDIANA'S PHARAOH

Willard Aldrich of Mishawaka, planning his own funeral, had a casket built so that he could be buried sitting up looking out a small window.

The coffin was destined for a grave just as unusual. The vault was a 10-foot-square room. Its walls were adorned with pictures of cowboys, horses, and beautiful women. Furnishings included a table holding a deck of playing cards, a bottle of whiskey, pipe, tobacco, and matches. There also was a saddle, a shotgun (Aldrich said this was to protect him from the devil), and boots—which he obviously did not have on when he died September 7, 1882 at the age of forty-two.

It was said that J. W. Martling, who built the special vault, was never paid. Which fits in with Aldrich's style; he obviously wanted to take as much as he could with him.

■ THE DESPERATE DESIGNER

Maybe Samuel M. Foster wouldn't have become a success if he hadn't been failing.

But this, his third business, a dry goods store at Fort Wayne, was facing disaster. It lacked two things—stock and customers. After a depressing season in 1884–85, Foster looked back on a single ray of hope. He had sold a lot of boys' shirts at nineteen cents each. If they wanted a boy's shirt, they should have it. What did the Yale University graduate have to lose? A degree-holder at twenty-seven, he had tried newspapering at Dayton, Ohio, and another dry goods business at Danville, Illinois. Maybe the shirts were his last chance.

A clerk brought in one of the garments his son had worn for months. Carefully taking it apart to obtain a pattern, Foster turned his clerks, who had no customers anyway, into cloth cutters.

The shirts sold well in surrounding towns where Foster sent his traveling salesmen, but the runaway success was size 14. Women were buying them for themselves. It seemed that boys' plain shirts were just the thing for their tennis and other leisure activities. Foster, acquainted with failure, seized success.

Within two years this garment, the women's shirtwaist, was doing well in stripes, polka dots, black and white, and colors. Sales spread everywhere.

And that's how this simple blouse-like garment—the top that later made the Gibson girl a Gibson girl—the style which never really died, was born in Indiana.

"It became the rage all over the country," Foster later told a questioner. "As far as I know, I was the pioneer manufacturer of the ladies' shirtwaist."

Dozens of variations evolved, until the close of World War I slowed the craze. Then the Foster Shirtwaist factory modified its business into dresses, meeting a new demand.

Foster operated his Shirtwaist Factory on East Columbia Street in Fort Wayne for years.

He had emancipated women from cumbersome fashions that made them a slave to dress. He had freed them for the tennis court, a liberation which lives today, long after most people have forgotten the designer inspired by desperation.

■ Knowing Beans about It

Indiana owes the existence of its profitable crops of soybeans to a Hendricks County agricultural experimenter who imported them in the belief they could be a substitute for coffee.

Adrian A. Parsons was considered a joke by some. But the joke is on them—he had an immeasurable influence on the nation's agriculture, even if the result didn't reach the table via the coffee cup, as Parsons had hoped, for soybeans have become an important food source for both humans and animals.

Family members reported that Parsons imported the first soybeans from Japan in 1886 or 1887. Experimenting first in the garden, he extended his testing until he was selling soybeans by the carload. For many years the U.S. Department of Agriculture kept in touch with Parsons to remain abreast of developments in his fields.

The first imported soybeans were Mammoth Yellow, which were acclimated to grow in Hendricks County. Later Parsons used Ito Sans soybeans, and eventually a strain called Mikado was developed and sold all over the Midwest.

A report on Parsons's soybean achievements appeared in the *Prairie Farmer* January 11, 1930, documenting his contributions to the food chain.

■ Corn on the Current

For nearly twenty years corn served to remind Michigan City of one of the most unusual shipwrecks in the rich history of Lake Michigan shipping.

It began Monday, October 26, 1888, when the steel-hulled *Horace A. Tuttle* left Chicago bound for Buffalo, New York. In tow was the schooner *Aberdeen*. At 11:00

P.M., battling a sudden gale, the *Tuttle* sprang a leak. Turning back was dangerous because of the possibility of a collision with the powerless schooner.

Soon the storm made the decision; the *Tuttle* was blown around, forcing the captain to cut loose the *Aberdeen* and set course for Milwaukee.

When a huge wave on Wednesday evening stripped the *Tuttle* of hatches, deckhouse, and yawl boat and when the hold of the 250-foot-long ship filled with six feet of water, the captain turned toward Michigan City. There the vessel went aground and soon broke up.

Everything on board was saved except the cargo—77,000 bushels of shelled corn. Michigan City residents scooped up some, but a lot vanished under the waves.

As late as 1905 residents swore that when a storm arose, the unpleasant odor of sour corn would rise from the waves, a repeated reminder of the shipwreck whose smash produced a telltale mash.

HARRISON THE FLAG WAVER ◼

If any one person is responsible for public display of the American flag and the pledge of allegiance, it would be Hoosier President Benjamin Harrison.

Harrison was inspired in 1889 when he went to New York for a mammoth celebration commemorating the centennial of George Washington's inauguration. Landing at the Battery, Harrison rode up Broadway to Madison Square, moved by the waving flags and the almost palpable patriotism in the air. He wondered what would happen to all the flags when the celebration was over.

At a banquet that night in the Metropolitan Opera House, Harrison said: "I think the children should be taught and we should remember that the flag is not simply a war sign but an emblem of government."

From this thought, Harrison developed his idea of flying the flag at schoolhouses and public buildings. In all parts of the country he spoke of the love of the flag and its symbolic glory.

"Perhaps you do not realize how great a part in patriotism you had in ordering our flag to go up on all public schools," wrote Mrs. John C. Fremont, widow of the first Republican presidential candidate. "The daily impression on young receptive minds makes this a precious habit—the nation's daily prayer—and you are seeing some of the results. Long after they are grown—and we have passed away—your thought will continue its silent teachings."

Francis Bellamy, a Boston editor, wrote the pledge of allegiance during the late days of Harrison's administration. Added to waving flags, it completed a patriotic ritual inspired by the only chief executive ever elected from Indiana.

Benjamin Harrison, the only U.S. President elected from Indiana, not only was responsible for the Pledge of Allegiance but also prompted the custom of flying the U.S. flag above schools and other public buildings. (File photo)

At the age of thirteen, Dorsch, as his family sometimes called him, had obtained his schooling in parochial classes run militantly by German priests and he was certain he had learned nothing.

In one respect he was right.

Dorsch and his family moving again to escape pursuing poverty, arrived in Warsaw, Indiana, where public school was far different from what the boy had experienced previously. Especially seventh grade, where English was taught by May Calvert. She opened a new world to Dorsch—literature. But not grammar.

The boy could not master the schoolroom rules of the language. He had come to seventh grade without the basics. He flunked. May Calvert kept him after school for extra help—to no avail.

"It was a profound mystery, no least rudiment of which I ever mastered—and when she gradually discovered that I knew absolutely nothing concerning it, she merely looked at me and pinched my cheek," Dorsch recalled later.

"Well, don't you worry," May Calvert said. "You can get along without grammar for a while yet. You'll understand it later on."

Slipping through to high school, the boy met Miss Mildred Fielding, the teacher who guided his reading in literary classics.

But at fifteen Dorsch quit, journeyed to Chicago, and went to work in a warehouse, fretting over his future. Miss Fielding, transferred to Chicago to teach, found the boy and insisted he accept $300 from her and use it to attend Indiana University. He did, for a year. But he realized that college didn't make much sense to him. "I think I failed in most things because I never mastered grammar or mathematics," he recalled.

At eighteen he was out in the world again. But as time passed, the memory of failing at grammar faded before his perpetually realistic outlook and his persistence at painting pictures with words. Grammar had failed him, but observation and creativity hadn't.

Dorsch was Theodore Dreiser, one of Indiana's most controversial writers. His books, including *Sister Carrie* and *An American Tragedy,* were debated by critics, banned and hailed for their content.

His drive to communicate had overcome his earlier inability to conjugate.

■ THE KOUTS BOUT

Maybe it was enough to box eighty-four rounds and still be able to walk away. Survival was about all that Ike Weir and Frank Murphy got for their title bout in 1889 at Kouts. The longest fight in Indiana history was a draw. The community was outraged. And in the end the Sabbath kept the fighters from answering the bell.

The featherweight world championship match had been set for Chicago between champion Weir, billed as the Belfast Spider, and Murphy, an English champion. But the Windy city refused to permit boxing in skintight gloves; the promoters refused to adopt four-ounce gloves, so an out-of-town site was sought.

Kouts, a small Porter County community, fancied some of the sporting life and the match was booked into Mike O'Brien's Hall Saturday, March 31. The justice of the peace was taken to Valparaiso on a bogus errand.

The charter train puffed in from Chicago carrying fighters, trainers and handlers, ring officials, promoters, and far more gambling ticket-holders than could fit into the hall. Some had to stay outside, getting the blow-by-blow from a megaphone through a window.

After sixteen rounds in the late-starting fight, neither

boxer had enough power left to win the $1,500 purse and the crown. But the fight had been billed "to the finish" so it continued because of the money that had been wagered.

When midnight came and went, Kouts citizens protested; they were shouted down. At sixty rounds, both fighters were sleeping between rounds. One had black eyes and blurred vision. The other had hands so sore from pummeling his opponent's head that he could no longer hit; he merely pushed.

By daylight ministers joined the protesters, pleading violation of the Sabbath. When ignored, they sent to Valparaiso for the sheriff. Fatigue, an excuse denied the exhausted fighters, struck the visitors; they were thirsty, hungry, and sleepy and wanted to get away before the sheriff arrived. The bout was called a draw at eighty-four rounds.

Although it was over the repercussions were not. Porter County newspapermen refused to report the details of the bout; it was kissed off as a "cruel and brutal exhibition." The Methodists were angry at Mike O'Brien, even though he had the hall tidied up in time for services. They deplored their church hall being used for brutality.

O'Brien was pragmatic. He reported he got more rent for that one night of boxing than he got in a year from Methodism.

Ike Weir, although he reportedly weakened a bit somewhere between the seventieth and eighty-fourth rounds, retained his title.

He Rode for a Fall ■

The high, crouching style used for years by jockeys was brought to horse racing by a Hoosier, once the toast of royalty, who died penniless and in disgrace.

James Forman Sloan, born in 1874 at Bunker Hill

near Kokomo, was nicknamed Toad, shortened to Tod, because of his size, which was to serve him well on horseback.

At fifteen Tod ran away from home, began working around stables, and was given the chance to become a jockey by John S. Campbell of Kansas City, Missouri. Tod introduced the idea of the "fast break"—forcing the pace from the start of the race to outdistance opponents.

Then one day he realized that wind resistance, a force in racing, would be reduced if he crouched, stirrups drawn up high, behind the horse's withers. His Monkey Crouch brought derision until Tod began winning race after race. Then others adopted the style.

In 1897 Sloan went to Europe where jeers turned into imitation after he had won twenty-one races in less than a year and was selected as a jockey for King Edward VII. In three years Sloan became the toast of British and Parisian horsemen.

In 1901 England made the stunning announcement that Sloan's license was revoked because of "activities with a gambling ring and other conduct detrimental to the best interest of horse racing." The sporting world was shocked. But the revocation was upheld everywhere. Sloan's racing days were over. Once worth $250,000, Tod lived high and invested unwisely until he died broke in 1933 in Los Angeles. Although gone and forgotten, Tod's contribution to racing, the jockey stance, survives as his memorial.

He was the model for George M. Cohan's musical *Yankee Doodle Dandy*.

■ THE BIGGER THEY COME

It made sense, in a way, for John Hanson Craig to open a restaurant in Danville. Who would know more about eating than someone who weighed nearly half a ton, the mastodon man, one of the heaviest citizens of Indiana, one of only three known people in the world to weigh more than 900 pounds?

Craig was one of several Hoosiers whose size made

John Hanson Craig of Danville was six feet, five inches tall and reached a top weight of 907 pounds. (Photo courtesy of the Guilford Township Historical Collection)

them remarkable enough to be circus headliners. Craig, in fact, married a woman from Hendricks County who weighed more than 700 pounds and was the Fat Lady for P. T. Barnum's circus.

But she was no match for Baby Ruth, who peaked at 815 pounds and was an attraction with Royal American Shows and Ringling Brothers Circus. Born Ruth Smith at Kempton, Indiana, about 1904, she had no ambition to follow the career of her mother, a circus fat lady. So Baby Ruth attended secretarial school and tried to work for a telegraph company. But she was too large for the equipment; she already weighed 400 pounds. Work as a stenographer in a lawyer's office was equally unsuccessful despite her use of a specially made chair; people kept barging into the office to look at her. So she ended up where her mother had been—with Ringling Brothers.

In the circus she acquired a husband, Joe Pontico, a balloon salesman in Madison Square Garden, who took one look at the 697-pound Baby Ruth and dubbed her "my woman." But Baby Ruth was distressed. Although reputedly earning $300 a day, she could not lead a normal life, and she continued to grow at the rate of forty pounds a year.

In 1942 she checked into a hospital at Tampa, Florida, to have tumors removed from the inside of her knees. Surgery was postponed when the hospital bed collapsed, but she returned with her own special bed and successfully underwent the thirty-minute operation. However, as she was coming out of the anesthesia, she started to disgorge and, since the nurses couldn't turn over her 800 pounds, she choked to death.

A bizarre death also came to Robert Earl Hughes, who was just passing through Indiana in 1958 on a tour with the Gooding Brothers Amusement Company. His mobile home, a reinforced semitrailer truck, made it possible for Hughes, who weighed 1,069 pounds at his peak, to travel and earn a living.

When Hughes contracted three-day measles, he was rushed to Bremen Community Hospital, since even minor illnesses can cause serious problems for people his size. Since he could not fit through the hospital's doors or into its beds, Hughes was compelled to stay in his trailer in the parking lot. Nurses, physicians, and technicians treated him there.

Although the measles cleared up, Hughes was then stricken with uremia. On July 10, a few days after he had parked outside the hospital, he was dead, at 1,041 pounds, the heaviest man ever to die in Indiana. He was taken to his native Illinois to be buried—in a coffin the size of a piano case.

Jack Eckert weighed a mere 739 pounds when he died after a traffic accident in 1939. Eckert weighed nineteen pounds at birth at Lafayette. At ten when he weighed 265 pounds, he went into show business, traveling with Barnum, appearing at the World's Fair in Chicago and at the Panama Pacific Exposition in San Francisco, using the name Happy Jack Eckert. In fact, he did greet his audiences with a smile, although he could not have been very joyful with an eighty-seven-inch waist.

Like Hughes, Eckert made his home in a truck which also was his showcase. He was in it en route to Mobile, Alabama, for the Mardi Gras carnival when there was a collision with another truck. It took ten men to load Eckert into the ambulance; in a few weeks he was dead at sixty-two of internal injuries and broken ribs; he had been a trouper more than half a century.

John Craig's life is well documented because he used Danville as his headquarters during years he traveled with the circus. He even tried to become an ordinary businessman there, opening a combination candy shop and lunch business on the town square. Then he tried establishing a zoo at his Danville home. Both ventures were only moderately successful.

Craig died June 25, 1894, in his Danville home, his

body carried off in a custom-made coffin six feet, nine inches long and thirty-four inches wide. A window had to be removed to get it out of Craig's house. After forty-seven years, the life of the heaviest Hoosier on record came to an end.

Craig, born weighing eleven pounds in 1847 in Iowa, tipped the scales at seventy-seven pounds by the time he was eleven months old. When two years old he won the weight title at 206 pounds in Barnum's Baby Show in New York, winning $1,000.

When Craig moved to Danville is not certain, but he was a familiar, and large, figure in the town during the 1880s and 1890s. He stood six feet, five inches tall and reached a weight of 907 pounds. His hips measured eight feet, four inches, his thighs were sixty inches around and his chest was sixty-five inches. Once Harry McPhetridge, a Danville tailor, displayed one of Craig's suits in his store window. Three Danville characters borrowed the suit, put it around all three of them and walked around the square.

As a teen-ager, weighing a mere 500 pounds, Craig toured with Barnum. There he met Mary Jan Kesler, daughter of a Hendricks County family, who weighed more than 700 pounds and was Barnum's Fat Lady. They married. After the ceremony March 30, 1869, the Craigs toured in their own traveling circus, using their show business names of Powers and French. They returned to Danville between tours.

When their home lunch business failed and fire destroyed the monkeys, macaws, snake, and gorilla in their zoo, the Craigs went back on the road. Mary Craig, in poor health and fatigued by travel, died October 4, 1881.

Back on the road alone, Craig met and married Jennie Ryan, a native of Tippecanoe County, a petite woman whose connection with the circus was unclear. Their union resulted in a child, Helen, in October 1890. In December

1892, Jennie sued for divorce, charging cruel and inhuman treatment. The divorce was granted in January 1893. Three months later the Craigs remarried. Jennie was twenty-seven.

In the spring of 1894 the Craigs separated; Jennie returned to her family in Tippecanoe. Craig died that summer. William Roddy, Craig's manager, took care of three-year-old Helen until Mrs. Craig returned to Danville to settle the estate. She and Roddy were soon married and she left the area. Later she became Mrs. F. O. Markle, residing in San Diego, California. What happened to her after that is unknown.

But it is certain she never matched the status of her husband—the biggest corpse ever put to rest in Danville's Mt. Pleasant Cemetery.

WAKE-A-BYE JONES ■

Maybe a lot of Indiana towns were sleepy communities before the turn of the century, but David Jones carried that concept to extremes.

Jones was an insomniac—one of the best, according to the newspaper in Anderson, where Jones lived. Its issue of December 11, 1895, reported: "David Jones of this city, who attracted the attention of the entire medical profession two years go by a sleepless spell of ninety-three days and last year by another spell which extended over one hundred and thirty-one days, is beginning on another which he feels will be more serious that the preceding ones. He was put on the circuit jury three weeks ago, and counting today he has not slept for twenty days and nights.

"He eats and talks as well as usual and is full of business and activity. He does not experience any bad effects whatever from the spell, nor did he during the

Ralph R. Teetor of Hagerstown; he built an automobile though blind. (File photo)

one hundred and thirty-one days. During that spell he attended to all of his farm business. He says now that he feels as though he will never sleep again. He does not seem to bother himself about the prospects of a long and tedious wake.

"Mr. Jones cannot attribute his abnormality to any one thing but thinks it was probably superinduced by the use of tobacco while very young."

■ SIGHT VERSUS INSIGHT

They say Ralph R. Teetor was inspired by the story of Thomas Edison in a book, *True Stories of Great Americans,* which his parents read to him about the time he started to school. The evidence showed early. Teetor quickly came to prefer the tools of his grandfather and uncle to the playthings of other boys.

By the time he was ten, Teetor had constructed a miniature dynamo to light his workshop, and had adapted a gasoline engine to drive a lathe on which he built wood and metal parts for his inventions. His favorite pastime was to dismantle and rebuild machinery.

In 1902, when he was twelve, Teetor found a discarded engine and used it to created a horseless carriage which he drove on the streets of Hagerstown. He made the simple, lever-type steering device and the tireless flat rim wheels.

When Teetor was graduated from high school in 1908, the commencement exercises took place under the town's first electric sign on the Odd Fellows Opera House stage. Teetor and some of his friends had built it from scrap and wired it into the new generator at the town hall.

In 1912 Teetor was graduated from the University of Pennsylvania with a degree in engineering. He was to obtain a master's degree from the same school in 1930.

In World War I Teetor, working for the New York Shipbuilding Corporation at Camden, New Jersey, devised a way to eliminate vibration in the turbines of torpedo boat destroyers which was so severe the boats could not be used. They were reactivated in World War II.

Returning to Hagerstown in 1919, Teetor, a partner in Teetor-Hartley Motor Company, devoted his time to piston ring manufacturing. The firm became Perfect Circle Corporation, later a division of Dana Corporation, one of the largest manufacturers of piston rings in the world. Teetor became chief engineer and was president of the firm from 1946 to 1957.

Inspired by the need to conserve gasoline during World War II, Teetor invented a cruise control for automobiles which was introduced in 1957 and sold under various names. His mechanical and electrical innovations included improved door locks, suitcases, an Easy Fish Rod holder, and a power lawn mower which was developed twenty years before they became generally popular.

Twenty-five years after his graduation, Teetor was asked to address the University of Pennsylvania engineering alumni on "Progress in the Automotive Industry and Development of the Auto Diesel Engines." His picture was chosen to represent all graduates of the mechanical engineering school at the university in the Gallery of Distinguished Alumni in 1975.

One thing sets Teetor's accomplishments apart. He was blind. In an accident when he was five a knife had destroyed one eye. The other eye was saved in surgery at Richmond, Indianapolis, and Cincinnati, but it was weak and quickly failed.

Despite it all, an orderly mind and an orderly workbench permitted Teetor to succeed instead of surrendering to the darkness.

■ PREACHING POWER

Long before evangelists turned to electronics to reach a large audience, Indiana had a preacher whose accomplishments were remarkable in a pre-television age. His name was William Ashley (Billy) Sunday. It is estimated that he preached to more than 100 million people in less than forty years without the aid of broadcasting, usually without even the help of a microphone.

Billy Sunday made Winona Lake near Warsaw his Indiana home from 1895 until his death in 1935. He returned to Indiana each summer after national tours and built a one-story tabernacle at Winona Lake that held 7,500 listeners. An acoustical saucer over his head carried his voice throughout the tabernacle. Taking its cue from

Sunday, Winona Lake became an unusual religious community with activities that included a summer normal school, song directors' school, mission school, and school of theology.

Sunday, born in Iowa, played baseball for a number of years and was "saved" at the Pacific Garden Rescue Mission in Chicago after he had been out drinking with baseball buddies.

He soon abandoned sports to work for the YMCA and then became an assistant to Dr. Wilbur Chapman, an evangelist. Sunday himself began evangelism in 1896. Soon he had a staff of eight, lived in a mansion provided by believers, and preached all over the country. His sermons were marked by plain but colorful language, often employing similes from the sports world.

Because of the sawdust used on the floor of his tabernacle to help with the acoustics, the term "hit the sawdust trail" was coined to describe those coming forth to be converted to Christianity. With an unamplified speaking voice, Sunday is estimated to have induced at least one million to "hit the sawdust trail."

From Horsehide to Cowboys ■

The baseball roster at Fort Wayne before the turn of the century contained a name that later became famous in a field far removed from sports.

The player from Zanesville, Ohio, came fresh from the University of Pennsylvania, where he had been successful in several sports. As a twenty-three-year-old on the Summit City team in the Interstate Pro League in 1896, he put a season batting average of .374 into the books.

Much later his name was to appear on more than 100 million different kinds of books, sold throughout the world in dozens of languages. The Fort Wayne baseball player was Zane Grey, more skillful in later years with a pen than with a bat.

■ THE HORSE SENSE THAT FALTERED

Probably no other horseman in Indiana—a state known for its experts on pacers and trotters—ever made a bigger mistake than John Wattles did.

Wattles trained and raced horses around Oxford in Benton County. It was there on April 29, 1896 that a colt was foaled which at first was a considerable disappointment to its owner, country storekeeper Dan Messner.

Messner had paired his dam, Zelica, with Joe Patchen, an outstanding pacer at Chabanse, Illinois. But the offspring, a mahogany-colored colt, had legs that bowed. He was ugly, or just plain awkward; observers varied in their opinions.

The townspeople, used to admiring the best in horseflesh, ridiculed Messner when he would take to the dirt and gravel lanes with Zelica hitched to a buggy. The mare's foal followed, sometimes falling far behind, his ungainliness exaggerated by his inexperience.

One day Messner met Wattles, as the story goes, and noted that the trainer himself also had a colt. "Trade you even, John," Messner is reported to have said. "My colt for yours." Wattles, probably allergic to the snickering that followed Messner and his colt, declined with vigor; nobody would unload such a critter on John Wattles.

The awkward colt was Dan Patch, considered by many to be the greatest pacer of all times, the only championship stallion never beaten in a race.

Wattles learned belatedly of his mistake from the seat of a sulky. When Dan Patch was four years old, Messner decided it was time to race him. He hired Wattles to drive the pacer in his first race at the Benton County

The Oxford, Indiana, home of Dan Patch. His record time is painted on the roof of a barn where he was stabled. An Oxford man had a chance to buy the horse, but declined. (Photo by the author)

Fair. Dan Patch won by an eighth of a mile. "He has speed all right, and he may have heart," Wattles admitted.

What Wattles had taken part in was the start of a nine-year career unmatched in racing. Dan Patch was sold after one successful season in 1901 to M. E Sturgis of New York City, who paid a then-high price of $20,000 for the horse. Messner sold because the poisoning of one of his other horses made him fear somebody was out to kill Dan Patch. Sturgis, in turn, sold Dan Patch in 1902 to Marion Willis Savage for a record $60,000.

Except for a few appearances at the Indiana State Fair and for exhibitions, the pacer never again returned to Indiana. Instead of John Wattles, Myron E. McHenry of Freeport, Illinois, was at the reins during most of the horse's career.

Dan set an unofficial mark of 1:55 for the mile and an official time of 1:55 1/4, a record which stood for more than thirty years. The horse's lifetime earnings were estimated at $2 million. The income included the proceeds from thousands of Dan Patch horseshoes. A cigar, numerous toys, a hobby horse, a washing machine, and a threshing machine were named for Dan Patch. People danced the Dan Patch Two-step. The horse was exhibited all over the continent, traveling 8,000 miles in 1907 alone.

Sturgis retired Dan Patch in 1909. The once awkward colt had become a superbly muscled bay, a perfect picture of an equine athlete, the toast of the pacing world.

So it was until July 11, 1916, when Dan Patch refused to lie down, appeared overcome by panic, and at last collapsed. They say he paced furiously, lying on his side, for half a minute, then died. His owner, Sturgis, who had been hospitalized in Minneapolis July 4, 1916, with a heart attack, died thirty-two hours after his famous horse died. Their funerals were held at the same hour; Dan Patch was buried on the Minnesota River farm, Sturgis in Minneapolis. Dan Patch's heart, examined in an autopsy, weighed nine pounds, two ounces, almost twice the size of a normal horse's heart.

John Wattles had been right, figuratively and literally. But whereas Dan Patch went to his grave knowing he was a champion, John Wattles went to his knowing he had missed that one chance in a lifetime to own the greatest pacer Indiana ever produced.

HAPPY—NOT SO FAST—BIRTHDAY ■

Edith Briggs of Fulton County lived the first eight years of her life without a birthday.

It happened like this: Edith was born to John and Carrie Burns at Grass Creek February 29, 1896. That made her a Leap Year baby. But there was no February 29 in 1900, which would have been her first real birthday anniversary. Century years not divisible by four are not Leap Years.

So Edith had to wait until February 29, 1904, to have her first official birthday anniversary.

That made her a member of the 8 Years without a Birthday Club, founded in 1964 by V. Milton Stone of California. There were 155 charter members. Edith Briggs once served as vice-president of the club's central area, Wisconsin, Illinois, Indiana, Michigan, Minnesota, Ohio, Tennessee, and West Virginia. Ten other members of the club lived in the area.

The Hoosier whose first happy birthday was not celebrated for eight years died on March 19, 1975.

THE HANGING JUDGMENT ■

Few crimes in Indiana surpass the bizarre case of Lyle Levi of Versailles who, according to the official report, broke into jail, shot himself, then killed and hanged four other men, and finally hanged himself to divert suspicion from the crime.

Considering the fact that Levi was a sixty-year-old counterfeiter and his "victims" ranged from twenty-one to thirty-five years old, this was a major undertaking somewhat out of character.

In fact, all five men were killed by angry Versailles citizens, aroused by outlaws who had robbed and tortured citizens of the area in 1897. Shortly after a farmer named Bultman was burned on the hands and feet with live coals, the sheriff seized and jailed Bert Andrews, thirty, and Clifford Gordon, twenty-one. Already in jail were Levi, William Jenkins, thirty-five, and Henry Schuter, twenty-eight.

A mob estimated at 400 seized the five the night of September 14 and the morning of September 15 left them in the cemetery hanging from an elm, later known as the hanging tree.

The sentiments of the town became evident when the coroner declared that the men somehow had obtained rope from the hardware store and hanged themselves. This was somewhat difficult to believe, since Levi had been shot and Jenkins and Schuter clubbed to death. So Governor James A. Mount ordered his attorney general, William A. Ketcham, to investigate. Ketcham filed a report March 2, 1898, which outlined details leading up to the deaths and then declared in part:

"That Lyle Levi, having been incarcerated in the jail, and not being satisfied with surroundings or associates, and knowing that Wilder Levi's revolver was at McCoy's store in Osgood, broke jail—it's not important in this connection to ascertain how he broke jail—and went to Osgood—the manner of his getting to Osgood is likewise immaterial—that he broke into McCoy's store, stole Wilder Levi's revolver, returned to Versailles, broke back into jail, without the knowledge of the guards, who apparently were asleep at their posts at this time, returned to his cell, shot himself, then killed Schuter and Jenkins and with a rope that he had got hold of somehow, but the evidence does not disclose how or in what place he obtained it—hung the dead bodies of Schuter and Jenkins to the tree, put the finishing touches to his crime by hanging Andrews and Gordon and then, in order that suspicion might be directed against innocent men, finally hung himself, and his nefarious conduct in attempting to distract attention from himself and divert suspicion to the good citizens of Osgood, Napoleon, Milan and Versailles, all of whom were in the habit of retiring to their beds (and followed that habit on this particular night), immediately after eleven o'clock at night—the hour at which, under the law, saloons are required to be closed—is the more reprehensible, as apparently nothing in his life so became him as the leaving of it."

No action ever was taken against the mob justice, which has become the most famous crime incident in Ripley County. Even today Versailles has a restaurant called the Hanging Tree Inn. But the tree is gone; souvenir hunters over the years dismembered it.

PREGNANT WITH PROMISE ▪

"This operation is very simple and easy to perform," wrote Dr. Harry Sharp of Indianapolis.

Dr. Sharp's report, published in the *A.M.A. Journal* in December 1909, outlined the surgery he began performing in October 1899. "I do it without administering an anesthetic, either general or local. It requires about three minutes time to perform the operation, and the subject returns to his work immediately, suffering no inconvenience, and is in no way hampered in his pursuit of life, liberty, and happiness, but is effectively sterilized."

Thus did Dr. Sharp perform the first vasectomies known in America. From 1899 to 1907 the operation was done on 176 men in the Indiana Reformatory.

Today millions of men have had vasectomies. But not for the reason Dr. Sharp had in mind.

His operations were designed not to provide sterility, but to halt sexual desires, something which it is known today cannot be accomplished by vasectomies. But medical science had a different view in 1899.

"A boy nineteen years old came to me and asked that he be castrated as he could not resist the desire to masturbate," reported Dr. Sharp. "I first had him put in a cell with a fellow inmate, thinking that perhaps he would be abashed and the sense of shame would prevent him. He came to me again still insisting on castration saying it was as bad as ever.

"I did the operation [vasectomy] and two weeks afterward he came to me and said I was just fooling him, that I had not operated on him and he wanted the other operation [castration]. I told him to wait two months and then, if he was no better, I would perform castration.

"In two months time he came to me and told me he had ceased to masturbate and that he was all right. I asked him if he had lost any desire or pleasure of the gratification. He said, 'No, but I have the will power to restrain myself.'"

Dr. Sharp's article was titled "Vasectomy as a Means of Preventing Procreation in Defectives."

■ FINGERS ENOUGH

Before the turn of the century there were few provisions for handicapped teenagers, so Mordecai Brown was forced to compete with the rest of the boys in Parke County. There had been plenty of time for him to get used to his crippled right hand.

Mordecai was less than six years old when his hand became caught in a corn cutter and his forefinger was severed at the second knuckle.

It didn't slow the boy down. In fact, while his hand still was in a cast, he chased a rabbit and tumbled into a rain barrel. Although he evidently felt nothing, when the cast was removed later, his second finger was broken and unrepairable and there was a permanent crook in his little finger.

At working age, Mordecai moved to Terre Haute and found a job in the nearby coal mines. And he played baseball. With no quarter asked or given, he joined other teenagers, hurling the ball with his remaining three fingers. He was good enough to enter professional baseball in the minor leagues, playing third base.

Legend clouds how it happened. Some say that Mordecai took the pitcher's mound for the first time when the regular pitcher failed to show up for a game. He only recalled that one day the coach said, "You're a pitcher," and Mordecai took his word for it.

However it happened, it soon became evident that the mangled hand was an asset. Because of it, Mordecai (Three Finger) Brown could throw a mean curve ball and a wicked hop.

He moved through the Terre Haute Three-I League team to the St. Louis Cardinals and finally became a pitcher with the Chicago Cubs. He pitched against the famed Giant hurler Christy Mathewson twenty-four times and beat him thirteen times.

The Cubs won the pennant three consecutive times—1906, 1907, and 1908. Brown turned in three World Series shutouts in his career, hurled six one-hit games, and in fourteen years established a record of 239 victories and 131 losses. He earned a place in the Baseball Hall of Fame in 1949 and was chosen by the Helms Foundation as Indiana's outstanding professional athlete.

"All I know," Mordecai said, "is I had all the fingers I needed."

■ THE MOSQUITO MARTYR

A courageous Hoosier volunteer proved that yellow fever was caused by mosquitos. For his trouble John R. Kissinger was rewarded with a pension of $12 a month.

It began in 1900 at Columbus, about eight miles from Havana, Cuba, where GIs in the Spanish-American War had battled yellow fever as hard as the human enemy. No one was sure what caused the fever, but Maj. Walter Reed believed it came from mosquitos. He and three other doctors launched experiments aimed at proving it.

When Reed called for volunteers, Kissinger, a young private from the small Wabash County town of Liberty Mills, was the first to come forward.

November 23, 1900, Kissinger and John J. Moran of Ohio were subjected to mosquito bites. Nothing happened.

Seven other soldier-volunteers were placed in a building containing all manner of filth and the clothing of men who had suffered the fever. Their experiment was to test whether contact alone could cause the disease.

Meanwhile, Kissinger received another mosquito bite. He began to show signs of yellow fever. This was the first provable link between the disease and the insects. During eight days when his body was wracked with the agonies of the fever, more than 200 mosquitos were allowed to bite Kissinger. They would be used in later experiments.

Kissinger, who recovered by New Year's Day, 1901, had proven Reed's theory. A war against mosquitos was launched at once. "No more courageous deed than his has ever been recorded in the annals of the United States Army," Major Reed said of Kissinger.

Discharged and back home in Indiana, Kissinger found in 1906 that the mosquitos had given him something besides yellow fever—malaria. A bout with that disease rendered his legs useless. Although he was too proud to ask the Army for a pension, even though his wife had to take in washing, friends filled out the papers and Kissinger received $12 a month.

One day when the cradle of a neighbor's baby began to fall, Kissinger threw aside his crutches and rushed to save the infant. After that he gradually began to walk again. By the time World War I arrived, he was well enough to speak at Liberty Bond drives.

By the 1920s, some national magazines, learning of Kissinger's sad plight, launched a campaign which persuaded the Federal government to give the faltering hero a $100-a-month pension and the Medal of Honor. Popular subscriptions resulted in money to buy a frame home for the Kissingers near Huntington.

But within a few years Kissinger had to give up his house for the Indiana Soldiers' Home near Lafayette. He donated his mementos to the Huntington Public Library.

In July 1946 his life ended in Florida. He had moved there, only a few miles from the scene of his heroic act. Kissinger died as he had lived most of his life, practically forgotten.

MOTHER'S INITIAL HELPER ■

When Frank E. Hering made his plea in the English Theater in Indianapolis on February 7, 1904, it was the first public suggestion that a day be set aside to honor mothers.

Hering, a professor at the University of Notre Dame, was speaking at a memorial service gathering of the Indianapolis Order of Eagles Aerie No. 211. After noting the history of the Eagles, he launched into a tribute to mothers, citing the goodness of motherly love and the importance of motherhood. Nationwide, a day should be set aside to pay tribute to mothers, Hering urged.

Soon the Eagles decreed that each aerie should celebrate Mother's Day; President Woodrow Wilson established a national day in 1914.

Hering, who said he was only saying what thousands of others thought, received the American War Mothers Victory Medal in 1929. Two years later a plaque was dedicated at the English Theater recognizing Hering as the "father of Mother's Day."

A co-founder of the official *Eagles* magazine, Hering edited it for thirty-five years. He served ten years on the lay board of trustees of the University of Notre Dame before his death on July 11, 1943.

■ DEAD CENTER IN THE ROAD

It's one thing to be buried exactly where you wish; it's another for your grave to hold out for 150 years against all manner of progress—including county road builders. But not everybody has descendants as determined as those of Nancy Barnett.

Nancy and William Barnett came to Johnson County about 1821, settling on three acres of land near Sugar Creek. Nancy always said she wanted to be buried where she could look over at the creek. So when she died—the cause of death seems lost to history—she was buried close to the stream. Eventually the spot evolved into a small graveyard.

But a path which led from a ford over Sugar Creek to Nancy's grave soon became Hill's Camp Road, which went right through the cemetery. As travel increased, all the graves were moved—except Nancy's. Legend has it that her son refused to let her grave be disturbed—it was beside the road and really not in the way.

But the years brought traffic closer and closer to the grave. When a bridge was built across Sugar Creek in

1905 and the road was widened, the grave was in the way. So was Willard Barnett, a relative of Nancy, who lived nearby.

Descendants swear that Willard met workmen at the

The grave of Nancy Barnett can still be seen in the middle of the road near Franklin. (Photo by the author)

grave with a shotgun, threatening that anybody who touched Nancy's final resting place would join her in death.

The workmen backed off and Willard went off to the county seat to make "legal arrangements." Whatever they were, Nancy's grave went untouched.

It still is today—right in the middle of County Road S 400, which politely forks and circumvents the marker, making it the only Indiana grave surviving in the middle of a road.

▪ WHEN SMOKING CAUSED SPARKS

Hoosiers urging restricted smoking in public places in the late 1980s and early 1990s may not recall that for five years Indiana law prohibited all smoking. And the state granted smoking rights to Hoosiers of all ages only as recently as 1977.

In 1905 forces aiding the Indiana branch of the National Anti-Cigarette League introduced legislation banning smoking under penalty of fines up to $500. On February 3 the bill passed the Senate and came before the House of Representatives nineteen days later. There Ananias Baker, a representative from Fulton and Cass counties, announced that tobacco interests had tried to bribe him to vote against the bill. His story, buttressed by money given him in a sealed envelope, put pressure on the politicians and the bill passed. Nobody wanted the public to think they were against the bill because they had been paid off.

The first significant victim of the law was John M. Lewis, fined $25 and costs at Anderson when he was caught smoking and cigarettes were found in his pockets. Lewis appealed to the state supreme court. The law was upheld.

Then in Indianapolis was found that monument to lawmakers, a loophole. Special Judge J. M. Leathers ruled in the case of Indianapolis attorney William W. Lowry that Lowry's offending cigarette had been brought into the state from Louisville, therefore was an item of commerce, and that the federal law of commerce superseded state laws. Import your smokes and use them in private and the law can't touch you, Leathers opined.

Five years later, in 1909, the smoking ban was ended for adults. The law was amended to apply only to minors. In 1973 it was changed to apply to persons younger than eighteen. In 1977 the ban was lifted entirely. Age restrictions were gradually added until today smoking is "legal" only for those over eighteen. And now, lawmakers are arguing about when and where smoking might be prohibited.

QUIET PLEASE, THIS IS AN ELECTION ■

Indiana politics has a long history of rough-and-tumble electioneering interspersed with periods of zeal for reform, and Martin County is no exception.

In 1906 the pattern of politics there was changed in a strange way never duplicated since in Indiana. Two candidates not only avoided speeches, refrained from soliciting votes, and made no promises, they even left the state during the campaign in accordance with a gentlemen's agreement.

Horace McDermed and Seymour Marshall, both experienced politicians, sought the office of country treasurer. It was a time of reform. The Democrats, Marshall's party members, offered a plan that would limit campaign expenditures and curb flagrant election abuses. But when reform faltered and sportsmanship appeared an imminent victim of partisanship, McDermed and Marshall created

their own cleanup effort. Their document, signed and no-
tarized, stipulated that each would move west of the Mississippi River by September 26, 1906, and not return to
Indiana until November 6, except in case of family illness.
Neither would spend money on a campaign, even in absen-
tia, nor would they solicit votes by mail.

The loser of the election would pay his opponent
$100 toward travel expenses and donate $100 to his
party's campaign fund.

The pair traveled together to St. Louis. There McDermed departed for a rest at Hot Springs, Arkansas, and
Marshall traveled to Springfield, Missouri, to visit relatives.

Back home the veteran politicians offered more heated
debate over the weird election agreement than McDermed
and Marshall would have had on the campaign trail, but
the two remained true to their vow.

It was a Democratic year; Marshall won by a comfortable margin, made the more comfortable because neither
man had wasted time, money, or energy on a campaign
that probably wouldn't have changed the outcome anyway.

After that, as far as history records, it was back to
politics as usual.

■ LEWDNESS AND A "G" STRING

Pupils were sneaking peeks at contraband books and com-
ics long before pornography became a cause—hiding them
in garages, barns, attics, or inside textbooks.

Cole Porter hid his in his violin case.

When the Peru, Indiana, native was sent by train
to the Marion Conservatory of Music, thirty miles from
his home, off he went with a violin case full of risqué
literature, penny novels called "dreadfuls." After his les-
son, he would read while waiting for the train.

He didn't master the violin, but he built up a rich storehouse of plots and phrases—including "Love for Sale," perhaps. At fourteen, the violin pretty well forgotten in favor of the piano, Porter found himself being questioned by the dean of New England's Worcester Academy about ditties circulating in the dormitory—such numbers as "The Tattooed Gentleman," "Fi Fi Fifi," and "The Bearded Lady." Porter admitted writing them. The lyrics of "The Bearded Lady" prompted the dean to suggest that Porter stop such musical creativity or face expulsion.

Luckily for later music lovers, Porter didn't stop composing often-bawdy songs. "I suppose," he said in retrospect, "some of my lyrics owe a debt to those naughty books."

LITTLE BIG-LEAGUE TOWN ■

What Hoosier city stands out as the main producer of baseball players for the major and minor leagues? Indianapolis, of course, has provided the most. But you have to reckon with Wadena.

This village in Union Township, Benton County, with a population near the turn of the century so small it could fit comfortably in a one-room schoolhouse, provided four baseball whizzes about the turn of the century. The town had organized its first local team in 1870.

Otis (Doc) Crandall was the first major leaguer from Wadena, starting with the New York Giants in 1908 to begin a ten-year career as a pitcher, notching 101 wins against 61 losses. He pitched in five World Series games. After leaving the majors Crandall pitched for another decade in the Pacific Coast League, a legend on the Los Angeles team.

While Doc was on the mound, brother Karl was playing for Indianapolis and Memphis in the Southern Association, a minor league. Another brother, Arnold, pitched for Buffalo in the International League.

Fred (Cy) Williams of Wadena reached the Chicago Cubs in 1912 and in four years had won a regular spot in the outfield. Because of his low batting average, the Cubs traded Williams to Philadelphia in 1917, only to see him top the .300 mark six out of seven seasons. In his best year he hit .345, surpassed in the league only by the great Rogers Hornsby. Williams was the National League home run king in 1920 and in 1923, when he tied the American League's Babe Ruth with forty-one four-baggers.

It was enough to cause cheering in Wadena, the Hoosier village that had to be the per-capita leader in producing baseball players—a feat accented by the fact that these baseball achievers started out on a team called the Wadena Plowboys.

■ Ballooning

If there was anything Carl G. Fisher liked better than fast cars and beautiful women it was hot-air balloons. He managed to spend a lot of time with all three.

Fisher, founder of the Indianapolis Motor Speedway and developer of Miami Beach, was an entrepreneur in Indianapolis, starting on his way to fortune with a bicycle shop. His business acumen and ability to spot a trend led him naturally to automobiles and he acquired one of the first car agencies in Indianapolis.

His promotional stunts included dropping a new car from the top of a downtown building to demonstrate the car's solid construction. He also floated a car over Indianapolis by balloon in 1908. Capt. G. L. Bumbaugh, Indianapolis pioneer balloonist, was Fisher's partner in the stunt. The car was attached to the balloon in place of the basket.

Several miles from town the balloon was landed, folded up, and replaced in the car, which was then driven back to town.

Fisher's wife, in writing his life story, revealed that he performed this eye-catching feat by using two cars. The one used as the gondola was stripped of its motor so it was light enough for the balloon. A second car had been taken out of town earlier. This was the auto driven back with the balloon inside.

Fisher also flew in one of the balloons that competed in a contest at the new Indianapolis Motor Speedway in 1909, the year it opened with a few auto races. The Fisher balloon traveled the farthest, but the victory was disallowed because Fisher and his companion had touched down in Tennessee.

Bumbaugh operated an Indianapolis balloon factory, which made more than 1,000 hot-air craft from soon after the turn of the century to 1936. He is credited with creating a sixty-five-foot-long Coca-Cola bottle balloon and balloons made to resemble a football, a golf ball, and a baseball. He also made the balloon that floated a piano over Indianapolis in the early 1930s—another Fisher stunt.

Gayle McDonald Sherwood was at the piano keyboard, but musicianship wasn't necessary. The instrument was a player piano, which the stunt was designed to advertise.

Mrs. Sherwood recalled that Captain Bumbaugh was the pilot for her piano flight. She and the piano were held inside by ropes. "We ascended from the Indianapolis gas works to about 3,000 feet where we stayed for about five hours," she recalled. "When it came time to descend, the captain lowered a rope to ease the piano down. They discovered we were over the New York Central tracks and that a fast train was due. Captain Bumbaugh started throwing sandbags over the side so that we could gain altitude and get away from that dangerous area. We then traveled all the way across the city to Irvington. Many people were there to help pull us down."

In recent times, an Indiana balloon incident involved irony and a tragedy.

Elizabeth Domont became the first licensed female balloonist in Indiana by passing a Federal Aviation Administration test August 30, 1977. Exactly one year later, she was killed when a balloon carrying her and two men hit a high-voltage wire east of Fishers, Indiana, just before sunset. She was photographing another balloon on its maiden flight when the accident occurred August 30, 1978. Mrs. Domont's balloon was named *Serendipity*.

■ PRISON INSIDE AND OUTSIDE

It wasn't an enviable record, the kind of thing Johnson Van Dyke Grigsby had sought. But he was always philosophical about it; given the circumstances, it was to be expected.

Grigsby lived sixty-six years in the Indiana State Prison, serving the longest prison stretch of any man anywhere in history, according to the *Guinness Book of World Records*. Grigsby, inmate No. 4045, was told he was free in November 1976. It was way too late. He had entered prison in a horse-drawn wagon on August 8, 1908. When he came out, he still was imprisoned mentally, too institutionalized to function. His years behind bars haunted him in the world of freedom. He ended his years living in the Marion County Health Care Center, the county home: it suited him because there he was told when to get up, what to eat, when to shave, bathe, and go to bed.

On December 3, 1907, in Alexandria, Grigsby stabbed the town bully during a dispute in a saloon. As a black man in those days, Grigsby knew he was lucky to be charged with murder instead of being lynched. He was sentenced to "natural life," and the state took the court at its word. He stayed behind bars until all his family members were dead, never even learning when some of them died. He had faded into the prison landscape.

Noticed eventually, Grigsby was paroled in December 1974 to a Michigan City nursing home, but he was back in prison in seventeen months. He had been upsetting the paying customers at the home, the first sign that it was too late to correct prison's imprint.

Grigsby could not be persuaded that the television performers were not real and invading his room—TV had been a science fiction fantasy when he left freedom.

A group of Indianapolis residents, hearing of Grigsby's plight, got Governor Otis R. Bowen to parole him to a one-room apartment at Thanksgiving, 1976. There he spent the time scrubbing the walls and floor, just as he had done for so long in prison. It was difficult to coax him from his room. He feared he would get in trouble for being away from his assigned place.

When his benefactors tired of fixing his meals, giving him his medicine, and tucking him into bed, Grigsby was moved to the county home.

There were times when Grigsby was cantankerous. Sometimes his thoughts wandered. But despite a lifetime seemingly without hope, Grigsby still believed in a future. He told a reporter: "I may take a notion to leave here some day. But I will never marry. When you have children they need to go to high school and college and the university and become preachers, lawyers, and doctors. Well, I just couldn't afford that school. I don't have any money, so I can't get married. Jesus never married, you know."

Grigsby died May 6, 1987. He was 101. He had survived thirteen years on the outside.

■ Cash on the Cob

A single ear of Indiana corn once sold for $250 at auction—and was purchased by its original owner, who decided the corn was valuable enough that it should be saved for his own use.

That ear was only slightly more unusual than nine other ears, raised by the same Hoosier, which brought a total of $1,000 in cash plus a trophy worth $1,000 and a new automobile.

The grower of this golden grain was Leonard B. Clore, who was so successful that the National Corn Association banned him from further competition in 1909. Clore's corn, Johnson County White Dent, won the international sweepstakes award at the Paris Exposition in 1900 and brought him $14,000 in prizes at various shows. At Chicago in 1909, his corn won the prize for the best ten ears and the best thirty ears, and then one ear was offered for bids. When the price reached $250, Clore bought the corn himself.

Over the years Clore's White Dent won him a 160-acre farm in Texas valued at $6,400, a piano, a stove, a watch, a clock, a mandolin, a lawn swing, and cash. He was so successful he received an offer (which he declined) to become Russia's corn consultant.

Clore also obtained many of the implements he used on his farm near Whiteland as prizes in contests won with the corn he found too valuable to let go to other auction bidders.

■ World Series Wonder

Babe Adams looked good on the pitcher's mound. He had coal black hair and piercing eyes, was a shade under six feet tall, weighted 180 pounds, and had the handsome outdoor look of a Tipton County farm boy, which he was.

But fans of the Pittsburgh Pirates were surprised that Adams was starting the opening game of the World Series against Detroit. Adams was, after all, a rookie. He had been used sparingly in the season and there was good question whether he had the experience for World Series combat, even if he did have a record of twelve wins and three losses.

But the fans were to see a lot of Adams during the 1909 battle for baseball's crown. Adams won that first game, 4–1. He came back in the fifth game and won that, too. In the seventh game, Adams again was on the mound; a Tiger never crossed the plate and the Pirates were world champions.

The fans had a new hero, one who was to pitch sixteen seasons in a career which included a twenty-one-inning game in 1914 when Adams never issued a base on balls. But he never was better than the autumn he did something no freshman pitcher had ever done before— win three World Series games.

Giving It the Gas ■

The automotive age dawned because a chemist in Indiana was willing to literally risk his neck to find a better way to extract gasoline from oil.

His name was Dr. Robert E. Humphreys. He undertook a job refused by veteran boilermakers and discovered the means of "cracking" the molecules of crude oil. Within a few years Dr. Humphreys's basic method made it possible to convert 52 percent of oil into gasoline, increasing the yield by five times.

In 1909 Humphreys was chief chemist for Standard Oil of Indiana, where he had worked for ten years. Told

Dr. Robert E. Humphreys, now deceased, conducted the world's first catalytic cracking of oil to produce high octane gasoline, as illustrated in the painting behind him. (Photo by the author)

to find a way to get more gasoline from oil, he and his assistants, Dr. F. M. Rogers and Dr. O. E. Bransky, first tried heat. "By passing vapors of heavy oil through heated zones we did crack the oils, but not sufficiently for our purposes," he recalled fifty years later. "The distillate had such a vile odor we knew that would never do. After trying quite a number of methods I turned to cracking it under pressure."

No one knew exactly how oil would react under heat and pressure. Possibly, as one historian noted, "the result might be a terrific explosion and loss of life."

A still was made, partly of bricks, and Humphreys began slowly building the temperature to 750 degrees and elevating the pressure. Boilermakers refused to repair the leaks created in the makeshift still. Dr. Humphreys had to clamber about on it, caulking the seams. "The still groaned and grunted, leaked here and there, and was cantankerous and perverse in many ways," he recalled.

The experiment succeeded. But the Standard board of directors were leery. When $1 million was sought for the first battery of stills, one director objected that the chemist "wants to blow the whole state of Indiana into Lake Michigan."

At last, $709,000 was allocated, and by 1913 a battery of twelve stills, each with a capacity of 8,250 gallons, went into operation at Whiting. The automobile age had arrived. Standard Oil sold rights to the cracking process to other processors in return for royalties, thus making possible the widespread manufacture of automotive fuel.

Dr. Humphreys was retired at sixty-five, devoting his time to photography and oil painting. He died in 1962 at the age of ninety-four.

In 1958 his leaky deathtrap of a still, rescued when the laboratory where it had been was razed, was reconstructed at the Smithsonian Institution.

What courage it took for that young chemist to face an explosive situation that scared off regular boilermakers! But it was a risk that paid off with creation of the era of the car.

JUDAH GOES TO THE MOVIES ■

Lew Wallace's book *Ben-Hur* made publishing history on more than one occasion. It was the first book to exceed the sales of the Bible. It was the first book to acquire the blessing of the Vatican. The book was even sold by Sears, Roebuck, which marketed one million copies at 39 cents each. And Wallace's story of the Christ, when translated onto the stage, became one of the longest running, most produced plays in history—and also one of the noisiest. In early performances, the sounds from a specially constructed treadmill used for the chariot race scene drowned out most of the dialogue. Despite that, the play was a success, with at least 6,000 performances in twenty-one years.

But among *Ben-Hur*'s most unusual accomplishments was to establish the movie rights of authors. Since the Supreme Court ruling in 1911, six years after Wallace's death, authors' works have been protected by "motion picture rights," a concept that prohibits movies being made from books without permission.

Such was not the case before *Ben-Hur*. Early movie makers merely borrowed a book's plot, put some actors on the set, cranked out the film, and released it to a public growing more eager every day. Nobody even knew for sure if there existed "rights" governing such use of novels.

The immense popularity of Wallace's novel inspired the Kalem Company to shoot a one-reel version at Manhattan Beach in New York. The movie, which had sixteen scenes, was released in January 1908.

The late Lew Wallace had always been protective of his book. He had resisted for some time even allowing it to be made into a play. Moreover, his son Henry Wallace, administrator of his estate, was no fan of early movies. Court action was inevitable.

The Wallace estate, along with his publisher, Harper, and the producers of the play, sued, charging the moviemakers with "unauthorized use of a valuable literary work." Kalem contended the movie was merely "a series of photographs." It was good for sales of the book and helped promote the stage play, they argued.

The final decision in 1911 rejected the Kalem claim. The film company was ordered to pay damages of $25,000. The action established for the first time the legal character of the motion picture as a dramatic and literary expression and set up the relationship between movies and novels, plays, and other written works.

In 1919 Henry Wallace expressed his continuing distaste for movies by placing a $400,000 price tag on film rights to *Ben-Hur*. A partnership took Wallace up on his offer, then put the rights up for sale in 1921 for $1 million. Instead, Goldwyn Productions persuaded the partnership to gamble on getting 50 cents for every $1 the picture might earn in the future.

The 1925 production, starring Ramon Novarro as Ben-Hur and Francis X. Bushman as Messala, was a smashing box office success, earning millions for the investors. Thus, *Ben-Hur* was not only the movie that created the role of rights holders, it also was the first movie to make a bundle for them.

A Congressman and His Dog ■

Few things more unusual than Representative Henry A. Barnhart's eulogy to his dog have been inserted in the *Congressional Record* by an Indiana congressman. Barnhart, a Democrat from Rochester, served in Congress from 1908 to 1919. This eloquent passage was put in the *Record* on April 29, 1912:

"A message from home today stating that old Bob, deaf and decrepit, but the family pet and pride and protector for fifteen years, had died, halted interest in all else with me save memory of the past; and while he was only a fox terrier dog, no affair of state, nor burst of congressional eloquence, nor dream of future glory attracts my attention, and I think and think and think.

"You were just a dog, Bob, but you were a 'thoroughbred' in your class, and if there ever was a faithful, alert, trustworthy, loyal, mind-your-own-business, self-respecting, gentleman dog, you were this illustrious 'dog-ality.'

"From the evening you came from Chicago a plump, little puppy to the hour of your death, the result of paralysis, superinduced by fighting two intruding Peru mongrels at the same time, you were the trusted watchman of our home, the devoted pal of the children, and my rollicking 'chum.'

"You could do stunts like the boys on land, in air, or in water; you showed many a pesky rat and prowling cat that life was not worth living; and the body scars you carried to your grave were so many badges of honor, for you never showed fear and never fought a dog smaller than yourself.

"No boy ever 'soaked' you or one of your young masters and 'got away with it' without being dog bitten; no man ever violently attacked you who didn't cry, 'Call off your dog'; and no one ever approached your home in an unseemly manner except to hear warning of your strenuous vigil or meet you face to face on the danger line of intrusion.

"Of course you occasionally erred in judgment. As I remember, you frightened Joe King into short growth, and you bit Uncle Adam Mow and Mike Henry and Huston Black and numerous other good men who called on friendly mission and found only you at home and you were not sociable with other people.

"But your mistakes were due to your loyalty to me and mine, and I'm homesick and heartsick in sorrow because I must bid you, game and companionable old fellow, this everlasting farewell.

"No friend ever stood with us so firmly and so unselfishly as you, and all you asked in return was to have the door opened forty or fifty times a day that you might rush out and chase some roving curs away, and an occasional bone or some crumbs from the table.

"And so your memory shall be cherished with us as long as time lasts. Your constancy, your self-denial, and your admirable activity in the everyday affairs of the youths about you, as they grew from childhood to man's estate, have been a help to me beyond expression, and if any fellow citizen ever mistakenly or maliciously classes me with your kind, I hope he may compare me with you, Bob."

A Tip of the Hat to . . . ■

One Hoosier who appeared in Robert L. Ripley's "Believe It or Not" was cited because of a hat, believe it or not.

Otto Kafader, sixty-six, who lived on Sanders Street in Indianapolis, had worn the same derby hat for twenty-eight years. So reported Ripley in his syndicated newspaper feature on the unusual in the world, which appeared in hundreds of publications.

The *Indianapolis Star* printed the Kafader item on December 12, 1912, on the comic page. A drawing showed Kafader as a round-faced fellow wearing, naturally, a derby. "I got him a soft hat once, but he just never wore it at all," Kafader's son, Robert, told a reporter.

Kafader and his hat shared Ripley's allotment of space with Gladys Sturtevant of Rome, New York, who was never late for school in fourteen years, and the revelation that the word "eternity" appears only twice in the Bible.

Here's to the Heat ■

Only one Indiana product can be identified by blindfolded people in more than 130 countries around the globe.

The familiar Coca-Cola bottle was designed in Indiana at the Root Company, Terre Haute. This is one of the early versions. (File photo)

It is one of the first things patented by the U.S. government because of its shape.

And it owes its existence to the fact that Indiana becomes so hot in summer that in the days before air conditioning some industries closed when the mercury rose to the torrid zone.

Such was the case in 1913 when a soft-drink company launched a sweepstakes contest to design a bottle which would set its product aside from competitors. Because of the heat, the Root Glass Company at Terre Haute had shut down.

So some of the top men in the firm were set to work designing a bottle for the contest. T. Clyde Edwards, the company auditor, searched the encyclopedia for inspiration and hit on using the shape of the cacao bean as a model. Alexander Samuelson, the Swedish-born plant superintendent and an expert in glass technology, translated the design into a bottle.

By 1916 it had been chosen as the best of the entries in the sweepstakes. With few modifications, it remains today one of the most distinctive shapes in the realm of bottles, shipped around the globe containing Coca-Cola.

LUMBERING GIANTS ■

Indiana once had the largest tree in the nation east of the Yosemite Valley, and a remnant of it still can be examined at Worthington in Greene County. In 1915 the sycamore was called the largest tree in Indiana and the largest deciduous tree in the nation.

Another Indiana sycamore, almost as huge as the Worthington tree, is preserved at Kokomo where it once served as a telephone booth. Although its trunk was larger than the trunk of the Worthington tree, the Kokomo sycamore did not have the overall grandeur.

The Worthington sycamore gained its record status as an entry in a large tree contest conducted by the *Journal of Heredity,* which brought 337 entries from all parts of the United States. Herman L. Hayden of Worthington, Herbert H. Sloane of Worthington, and Dr. William B. Clarke of Indianapolis submitted the sycamore and won the $100 prize for themselves and championship status for the tree.

It measured forty-five feet, three inches in circumference a foot above the ground. One main branch was twenty-seven feet, eight inches in circumference and the other was twenty-three feet, two inches in circumference. A portion of the smaller branch has been preserved in the park at Worthington.

The tree grew in White River bottomland about one

The trunk of the giant tree preserved in a Kokomo park was once used to house a telephone booth. (Photo by the author)

and a half miles east of Worthington where the overflow of water repeatedly deposited loam at its feet. It was speculated that the loam contributed to its size. At times the flood waters reached as high as the fork in the tree, fifteen feet above the ground, according to witnesses. By 1915 the sycamore had reached an estimated age of 500 years. It rose 150 feet above the ground and some thought wind and lightning may have reduced its height. Its branches spread 100 feet.

In 1926 wind downed the tree. A portion of the smaller of its two main branches was saved and is displayed upright, protected by a roof, its openings plugged by concrete against further weather damage.

The tree that survives at Kokomo in Highland Park originally grew on the Tilghman Harrell farm about seven miles west of Kokomo. It was more than 100 feet tall and had a stump fifty-one feet in circumference.

A limb from a giant sycamore is displayed in the park at Worthington; it once was the largest known tree east of the Rockies. (Photo by the author)

In 1915 or early 1916 the tree was damaged in a storm. Jacob Bergman, then commissioner of the Kokomo park, thought the stump was worthy of display. A twelve-foot section of it was pulled to its present location by James Milner, a house mover. For a time its hollow inside served as a telephone booth.

Now enclosed by a new shelter, the stump bears hundreds of initials, names, and other markings inscribed in it by the countless visitors drawn to this remnant of one of the state's giants.

Observers point out that there have been even larger sycamores in Indiana, but they did not survive into this century like the Worthington and Kokomo sycamores. One such tree, which grew in Jackson County, had a circumference of more than sixty-seven feet.

Another giant Indiana tree was noted as early as 1867, although only its trunk existed at that time. It grew on the bank of the east fork of White River about three miles southeast of Brownstone in Jackson County. The stump showed that the tree had been sixty-seven feet in circumference.

Of all the giant trees that once grew in Indiana, only the Worthington and Kokomo sycamores have left remnants as memories.

■ PLANTED THEN, DUG LATER

John G. Coulter didn't invent the garden. But he did apply it to wartime. So the Victory Garden, devised during World War I, was a Hoosier invention although it didn't become an international passion until years later in World War II.

Coulter, a graduate of Indiana University, had established some reputation as a botanist before joining the Yanks in France in World War I as a private. His uncle, Stanley Coulter, had been a botanist and a dean at Purdue University. When Gen. Charles G. Dawes, commander of the service of supplies for Gen. John Pershing's armies, asked Coulter what he would do to improve conditions at the front, Coulter replied: "Raise fresh vegetables and send them up with the chow."

"You botanists," snorted the general. "If you had your way, you'd grow geraniums on the front line parapets."

But the seed had been planted—so to speak—and Coulter was soon summoned to Paris and told to establish a fresh vegetable section in the service of supplies, at first using plots around Versailles, not far from that city's famous gardens. Prisoners and recuperating soldiers were put to work in vegetable production.

"I tramped all over the French countryside, leasing

or buying outright thousands of acres of farmlands," Coulter said.

The first truckload of produce sent to the front was blown up by a German shell. Other loads were stolen en route by soldiers hungry for fresh additions to the rations. After that the vegetables were transported under tarpaulins imprinted with "Danger—High Explosives."

World War I was suitable for Coulter's vegetable convoys because it was stabilized, using trench warfare.

After World War I Coulter became manager of one of the largest estates in the country, at Beauvaise near Paris. He wrote half a dozen books, including one on French history. He vacationed occasionally in Indiana.

His return to the state came after the Nazis overran France, taking possession of his own modest farm near Paris. Back home, he became secretary of the Indiana committee for victory, and saw the concept of victory gardens adapted to help support mobile fighting in World War II and to bolster the spirits of home-front civilians beset by shortages.

PAINTING BY NUMBERS ■

William A. Bixler of Anderson did 5,000 paintings—all of the same scene.

Soon after completing his art training, Bixler, thirty-six years old, painted the scene described in James Whitcomb Riley's 1882 poem, "The Old Swimmin'-Hole," on the Brandywine River at Greenfield, where Riley grew up. He sent the painting to the famous poet.

When Greenfield proposed a statue of Riley, they found the sculptor's $16,000 fee too much for the city budget. But Bixler came to the rescue with a plan. He volunteered to give a copy of his swimming hole painting

Two versions of the 5,000 "Old Swimmin'-Hole" paintings done by artist William A. Bixler. How many still survive is unknown. A speed painter, Bixler prided himself on being able to complete a painting in only a few minutes. Although details varied, the overall image was always similar. (Collection of the James Whitcomb Riley Museum, Greenfield)

to any school where children contributed to the Riley statue fund. Schools all over the country responded.

By the time the statue was dedicated to America's school children in 1918, Bixler had repeated his painting, with slight variations, 5,000 times.

He estimated he had covered three million square inches of canvas with the paintings. He painted many other pictures, but none of them was repeated as often as the old swimming hole, a scene he eventually grew sick of putting on canvas.

The statue of Riley still stands in Greenfield's courthouse square.

What's in a Name? ■

To most, the name of the Shades State Park indicates the heavy forest growth that casts dark shadows, the gorges so deep and steep that even the noon sun is denied penetration. But the name really comes not from gentle nature's canopy but from a grisly scene of violence enacted shortly before Indiana became a state.

A pretty, young blonde pioneer wife, married to a drunkard who beat her and threatened her life, turned the tables one day. Waiting until drink put her mate to sleep, she seized the ax he had sharpened for her death and killed him with a blow to the head.

Years later a Hoosier told the story to Mary H. Krout, a reporter for an Indianapolis newspaper. She revealed the tale in 1919.

Her informant as a schoolboy of ten had heard the quickly spreading news of the slaying and had gone with fellow pupils to watch the victim's burial. The murderess, seventeen, told her tale of abuse and went free. She moved to another state.

As far as anybody knows, the skeletal remains of the victim still rest somewhere in the park today. For years the region in Montgomery and Parke counties had been called the Shades. And there had been no reason not to call it the Shades as a state park—even if that nickname stemmed from a longer, macabre phrase, the Shades of Death.

The Dunes Flower Child ■

There were two unusual things about the hermit who lived in a shack on the Lake Michigan dunes near Miller in Porter County during the early 1920s. The first was that the hermit was a woman. The second was that the woman hermit took a mate, another recluse almost as mysterious as she was.

The press dubbed her Diana of the Dunes, even after they knew she was really Alice Mable Gray, daughter of a Chicago physician, well educated, Phi Beta Kappa, a graduate student at the University of Chicago. Discontent had spurred the thirty-five-year-old Diana to leave the campus in 1915 and move into an abandoned fisherman's shack. She liked to skinny-dip in the lake, and her bronzed body attracted offshore fishermen like a flashing lure. An irate wife who marched up to Diana's beach hideaway to discuss the activities of the nude nymph was drive off at pistol point.

The thwarted wife tipped off the press, reporters stalked Diana and learned the story, and she became a headline.

"In solitude when we are least alone," a line from Byron, had guided Diana to the hut she called Driftwood, there to exist with little more than a jelly glass, a knife, a spoon, a blanket, and two guns. She slept under the stars sometimes. She made and sold boxes of driftwood. "My salary when I worked was nothing extraordinary, and yet here I have lived all winter and summer on the last pay envelope that I received in Chicago," she told a reporter. "I buy only bread and salt."

Evidence on Diana's past career was sketchy. There were unproven reports that she had worked as a secretary both at the University of Chicago and at the university's publication, *Astrophysical Journal*.

Paul Wilson, a kindred dune spirit, met Diana in 1920, perhaps during one of her occasional walks to Porter or Baillytown for supplies. Wilson was a fisherman, some said. Others said he was a Texas rattlesnake hunter who had read about Diana, or an industrial engineer, or a pugilist. One report had it that his name was really Izenblater and that he had spent six months in prison for stealing chickens. It was easy to believe that he must be guilty of other crimes as well and was looking for a hideout. Perhaps sharing feelings of rejection and indignation against society, the two recluses wed in 1921. They moved into a shack christened Wren's Nest.

Marriage complicated lives already difficult. Sightseers multiplied, to Wilson's irritation.

In 1922 the body of an unidentified man was found on the beach; Wilson was an immediate murder suspect. Evidence that the killing had occurred elsewhere saved him. A fight with a deputy sheriff over charges that the recluses had been looting empty cottages left Wilson shot and Diana with a skull fracture; the case was dismissed when it was found the deputy had been drinking.

Civilization crowded the pair. Their shack was in the middle of a proposed housing development which eventually became Ogden Dunes. The couple wanted to flee to Texas, but attempts to get their boat there via connected waterways failed; once they reportedly reached New Orleans, but for some unexplained reason came back to the dunes. Necessity mothered their surrender of some privacy. Diana guided nature tours. Wilson fished and built and sold rustic furniture.

On February 8, 1925, Wilson sought a doctor for Diana, who was ill with uremic poisoning. But she was beyond help; near midnight she died.

Wilson was dissuaded from his desire to place her body on a dunes pyre. But he couldn't attend the more traditional funeral service because he was in jail. He had broken down at her casket, then become infuriated at a reporter's question. He had whipped out a gun and fired wildly. Nobody was hit, but Wilson was jailed to "cool off." Meanwhile, his wife was buried in Oak Hill Cemetery in Gary in a grave unmarked today.

Released, Wilson packed up and vanished. Some say he first set fire to Wren's Nest. Others report he sold it to a neighbor, who burned it. The ten-year tale of the strangest hermits ever to seek seclusion on Indiana's dunes had come to an end.

■ The Center Who Carried His Load

The first and only official example of piggy-back basketball in Indiana was displayed by two players for the Butlerville Bulldogs in 1923. A change in the rules quickly made their stunt illegal.

Coach Herb Whitcomb cooked up the play, but warned the players to use the backboard when they shot the basket; he figured that dunking the ball would be illegal.

Raymond Rees, the Bulldogs' center at six feet, four inches tall, weighing 240 pounds, practiced the play with Merlin Swarthout, a five-footer who weighed 110 pounds. When Swarthout could fake out his defensive man, he would run to Rees, clamber on his shoulders, and take a pass from one of the other players. From atop Rees's shoulders it was a cinch for Swarthout to dump the ball into the basket out of reach of the defensive players.

The first time the Butlerville team tried the piggy-back play was against Scipio. They won. In the sectional tournament they used the stunt against Hayden, winning 36–13. Against Vernon the outcome was in doubt until the piggy-back went into effect; final score, Butlerville 16, Vernon 15.

Arthur L. Trester, head of the Indiana High School Athletic Association, was asked about the play. A search of the record books showed there was nothing to prevent piggy-back shots.

The Butlerville stunt brought articles in newspapers all over the United States—and a change in the rules.

These days players may dunk with impunity, but they have to stay off the center's shoulders when they shoot.

VICTIM AND SURVIVOR ■

Both the last surviving Civil War mother and the last soldier killed in that war were Hoosiers.

Mrs. Sarah Jane Asbury of Farmersburg outlived all others whose children served in the Civil War. Born in Kentucky in 1826, she came to Indiana when she was nine and later married the Rev. George W. Asbury. Their son, E. K. Asbury, served in the Civil War.

In 1926 Mrs. Asbury, better known as Aunt Sally, was granted a pension as the mother of a Civil War soldier, the only act of its kind by Congress. A year later, November 4, 1927, on her eighty-sixth wedding anniversary, Mrs. Asbury died at the age of 101. Her son, then eighty, survived, as did twenty-two grandchildren, fifty-nine great-grandchildren, and eight great-great-grandchildren.

The last man killed in the Civil War was Pvt. John J. Williams of Portland, whose death on May 13, 1865, came, by some accounts, after the war was over. Gen. Robert E. Lee and Gen. J. E. Johnston both had surrendered before Williams's unit opposed a large force at Palmetto Ranche, Texas.

The 34th Indiana Infantry was driven three miles in the encounter. Union casualties were eighty-two men killed, wounded, or taken prisoner. Williams was the last to fall.

Little is known of Williams. He was a twenty-one-year-old Jay County blacksmith when he joined up on March 28, 1864. Company records show he was hospitalized at New Orleans, but give no reason and reveal that his unit was hauling wood on Padre Island in January 1865.

The record of Williams's activities is blank from then until he became the 646,392nd—and last—Union soldier killed in battle.

■ IMMOVABLE FORCE, IRRESISTIBLE OBJECT

You could say one thing about Owen (Donie) Bush of Indianapolis as a major league baseball team manager. Once he made a decision, he stuck to it.

Bush's Pittsburgh Pirates made the World Series in 1927, helped by Hazen (Kiki) Cuyler, a twenty-five-year-old outfielder who batted third in the lineup. But shortly before the series, Bush decided to move Cuyler to the No. 2 batting spot. Cuyler, a superstitious sort, feared that would jinx him; he refused to bat second.

So Bush refused to play him. Cuyler would stay on the bench, said Bush, until he agreed to bat No. 2 and also admitted publicly that he liked the idea.

Cuyler and Bush were stubborn. Although Cuyler finally greed to bat No. 2, he refused to say he liked it, and Bush kept him on the bench. From that vantage point Cuyler saw the New York Yankees win the series in four straight. So far as anybody knows, he is the only top outfielder fit to play who ever sat out an entire series.

Cuyler went from there to the Chicago Cubs and eventually to the Baseball Hall of Fame. Bush was memorialized when the stadium home of the Indianapolis Indians was named for him.

■ HOT TIME IN THE OLD STATE

Indiana did one of the longest slow burns in history. It started in July 1927, in grass along U.S. 24 just east of Huntington. Maybe a carelessly tossed cigarette was to blame. A wisp of smoke rose over the grassy field, too insignificant to attract much attention at first. The smoke continued for hours. Then for days, then weeks, months. Still there was no open flame.

But as summer passed the underground progress of the heat could be marked in the small trees, shrubs, and bushes killed as their roots were burned. Fall came and the pall of smoke added a ghostly air to the field, suitable for a rural Halloween. As time passed the word spread about the underground fire, confined in a small deposit of peat, burning slowly downward. Interest was piqued when, as winter after winter passed, snow and rain had no effect on the ever-present smoke. Mild spring flooding did nothing to stop it.

For years sightseers came, watching the smoke rise and trying to imagine what was mysteriously happening underground.

In February 1939, the smouldering stopped. The deposit of peat, measuring an estimated 30 by 100 feet, no longer was afire. The slow burn of Huntington County was over after nearly a dozen years.

THE UP AND DOWN TOUCHDOWN ■

When Robert W. Fribley scored a touchdown for Logansport High School in 1930, he did it the hard way—by running 190 yards.

It happened on October 11 when Lafayette Jefferson High School hosted Logansport at 10:00 A.M. to avoid being overshadowed by a Purdue University game in the afternoon. Logansport had a good season to protect; it had won five in a row.

Among Logansport's players was Fribley, son of a Methodist minister, a nimble 198-pounder who stood six feet, three inches tall. He had played fullback two seasons at Elkhart and was now competing in his senior season. As a quarter miler in track competition, Fribley was noted for his long stride, and today he was to do some unusual running on the gridiron.

Both teams scored early. Logansport got a second touchdown just before halftime. After the intermission Logansport took possession when Lafayette kicked the ball to the Logansport two-yard line. The ball went to Fribley on the first play from scrimmage.

He headed upfield, reaching the forty-five-yard line. The opposition closed in. Fribley dodged, twisted, sought daylight, and when he found it, he was headed back toward his own goal. As the defense backed off, chasing him with caution, Fribley reached his own end zone.

A Jefferson player dived at him in the end zone, but missed. Realizing what had happened, the Logansport back turned upfield again. He broke into the clear at the thirty-five-yard line and, with the field in disarray, there was no stopping him until he reached the correct end zone.

Score: Logansport 19, Lafayette Jefferson 6.

Lafayette scored again, but the Fribley run had decided the game. Logansport went on to complete its nine-game season unbeaten.

Fribley went on to DePauw University, where he was on the all-state college team and ran the quarter mile in a time of 48.5 seconds. After three years in the Navy, he became a preacher, working at Richmond and Anderson and recalling the day he scored when it appeared he didn't have a prayer.

■ REACH OUT AND SHIFT SOMEONE

In today's schizoid world of telephone service, it is unusual enough to go twenty-nine straight days without some kind

Photo A: The Bell Telephone Building has started on its turn. Note the "hall" connecting it to the curved sidewalk. (File photo)

Photo B: The building has been turned so that it now faces north. Some of the gear required to make the move can be seen as well as the wiring used to keep everything in service. (File photo)

of disruption. But giving an entire telephone building a ninety-degree turn and then moving it another hundred feet in a month without any service problems calls for a real operator.

It was another era—1930. Indiana Bell Telephone needed more space in downtown Indianapolis. It decided to acquire it by moving its eight-story building to adjacent lots and constructing a new building where the old building had stood.

Why? Cost. Moving the building instead of demolishing it to make way for a new one would save the $800,000 value of the old building and avoid replacing $1 million worth of equipment. At a cost of $305,000—a lot of money in those days—this is how Bell was shifted:

The basement was emptied. Gas, water, and sewage connections were equipped with flexible hoses. Electrical power service was placed on wires with slack. Seven cables were spliced into the telephone circuits and given 200 feet of extra cable.

After two buildings were razed on the target site, a concrete slab was poured, topped with fir timbers on which were placed 800 tons of steel rails. This was the bed for the new location.

A system of jacks, I-beams, and rollers was placed beside each of the fifty-nine steel columns supporting the building. The entrance to the structure was connected to an arc of sidewalk by a movable steel bridge.

When all was ready, the jacks raised the columns a quarter inch off their foundations, the columns were cut away, and the weight of the building was transferred to thirty-six-inch steel rollers—4,000 of them. The building was ready to move.

A team of eighteen men manned the rollers. At a given signal, six pumps were simultaneously given to each horizontal jack. This moved the building about three-eighths of an inch. The building could be moved fifteen inches an hour, or up to eight feet a day.

Workers inside the building felt nothing. The only way they could measure movement was by the subtle shift of landmarks outside the windows. A 300-seat grandstand was built outside for spectators.

The building was moved until its east-facing doors were facing north. Then it was moved a short distance west to its new home.

The Eichleay Corporation of Pittsburgh, Pennsylvania, did the work, which was completed on November 12, 1930. Today, said an official of the Eichleay firm, such an operation would cost more than $300 million.

Bell built a new high-rise structure on the site vacated by the move, completing it in 1932. In 1964 the building that made moving history was torn down and replaced.

DEAD MEN HAVE TALES ■

Gangster John Dillinger already had died once before he was shot to death outside a movie theater in Chicago.

Dillinger and some of his gang were hiding out when he got the idea that changing his appearance and eliminating his fingerprints might help him elude the law. He and Homer Van Meter of Fort Wayne, his No. 1 machine-gunner, visited Dr. Harold B. Cassidy and Dr. Wilhelm Loeser in Chicago.

For $5,000, each man was to undergo surgery to change his appearance and mutilate his fingerprints,.

During the surgery Dillinger received an overdose of ether and was clinically dead. Said FBI director J. Edgar Hoover later, "It was only through the prompt action on the part of Loeser that he was resuscitated."

Dillinger was killed nearly a month later, July 22,

1934, when Melvin Purvis and fellow FBI agents shot him outside the Biograph Theater.

The plastic surgery long has been a point involved in the never-ending dispute over whether the man killed by the FBI really was Dillinger.

■ Husking Corn for 200,000 Ears

There was a time in Indiana when more spectators turned out to watch a corn husking contest than crowd the largest of Indiana stadiums for a November football game even today. Pictures of the national husking competition at Newtown in Fountain County show a crowd estimated at 100,000. The action was as impressive as the size of the audience. Five of the sixteen huskers broke the husking record.

It had been ten years since the national husking competition had been held in Indiana. The farm of Leslie K. Mitchell was the site on February 8, 1935.

Many in the crowd favored Lawrence Pitzer, who was from Fountain County and had won the Indiana championship. The other Hoosier entry was William Fields of White County, who was second in the state contest. The first and second place finishers in eight state contests were competitors in the Fountain County husk-off.

In anticipation of the crowd, two fifty-acre fields were set aside for guests, with more parking established as far away as two miles. Visitors were hauled from parking sites to the fields in school buses. Two fields were reserved for those arriving by airplane. Enterprising pilots offered rides over the fields during husking.

Rules were simple: the winner was the man husking the most corn in eight minutes, tossing it into a wagon. Wagons were equipped with "bangboards" of wood; they rose higher than the wagon and enabled ears to be "banged" into the wagons from one side much like a basketball plopping off a backboard.

Elmer Carlson of Audubon, Iowa, won, husking 41.52 bushels of corn. His prize was a trophy and $100. Pitzer finished third, husking 38.84 bushels in the allotted time. Three others bested the old record of 36.09 bushels, established in 1932.

The size of the crowd can be judged by the refreshments ordered: 1,800 pounds of beef, 1,500 pounds of wieners, 50,000 regular buns, 1,500 long buns, 8,000 doughnuts, 2,000 loaves of bread, and 1,700 pounds of coffee. As far as anybody knows, all the food disappeared.

So did most of Leslie Mitchell's corn. He complained later that nearly everyone in the crowd took an ear of corn as a souvenir. This, plus the damage to his property, made him the sole loser in one of the best-attended rural events ever held in Indiana.

It Was His Funeral ■

L. F. Bailiff preached his own funeral sermon.

On June 14, 1936, about 1,000 friends and neighbors assembled on the thirty-nine-acre Knoll Cove farm of Bailiff near Williamsport. As they picnicked, they listened to his talk on "To know one's self is wisdom; to govern that self is strength."

Bailiff, eighty years old, said, among other things:

"I don't know where we go from here and I don't care. Whether to heaven or hell I haven't had time to figure out. I do all the kindness I can here, and I'll take my chances."

He asked that his body be put on a pile of logs which should be set afire. Whether his wishes were carried out when he finally died seems lost in history.

■ CALIGULA, IL DUCE, AND A HOOSIER

That Shirl Herr of Crawfordsville invented what may have been the world's first metal detector is intriguing. That it was used to find artifacts at Fort Necessity, Yorktown, Fort Niagara, and Jamestown links it with history. That Admiral Byrd used the device on his second polar expedition to find equipment left behind during the first trip lends adventure to Herr's metal detector.

But nothing done by his "magnetic balance" surpasses the day Herr and his equipment helped Benito Mussolini find artifacts lost for ages in the muck at the bottom of Lake Nemi, thirty miles from Rome.

Herr, once honored as Crawfordsville's most useful citizen, found that his name had come to the attention of Mussolini, who was attempting to solve an unusual problem.

The Italian dictator was trying to raise the barge of Emperor Caligula in hopes that it would be a tourist attraction to aid Italy's flagging economy.

The vessel, used by Caligula for summer orgies, had been lavishly appointed with marble fountains and gold figureheads. One night the mad emperor fled his barge and had it sunk with all the artifacts and drunken guests on board. There it lay in the soft, black, tar-like bottom of Lake Nemi, the only known vessel surviving intact from Roman times.

Engineers drained Lake Nemi, but another problem demanded the expertise of Hoosier Herr. The barge had tipped, spilling many of its treasures. They now lay in four to five feet of semi-liquid bottom, kept in that state by the springs which were the lake's source and could not be shut off by engineering.

Herr was invited by Mussolini to bring his metal detector to Rome. Conducted to the site by the Italian leader himself, Herr worked from plank walkways over the lake muck. His son, Remley, carried the battery box that powered the detector.

Many items, including gleaming gold figureheads, were located by Herr, adding to the realism when Mussolini restored the barge, positioned so it appeared again to be sailing atop the lakes waves—but not for long. When the Nazis were fleeing Rome in World War II, they destroyed the Caligula barge and all the artifacts the man from Crawfordsville had helped resurrect.

ANIMAL ANOMALIES

Totts, the six-year-old Jersey cow of Paul Wesling of Rushville, made the movies in 1936. A film was shot showing the cow's ability to pump water for herself. She was pastured in a ten-acre field along U.S. 52 between Rushville and New Salem. There, probably because she was so far away from human aid, the animal had learned to use her nose to push up the pump handle and use her curved horn to fit around the handle and push it down.

* * *

At Berne in October 1948, the Holstein cow of Edwin Nussbaum made the news by giving birth to quadruplets, something agricultural authorities said occurs only about once in 500,000 times. The three heifers and a bull were alive and strong and each weighed about fifty pounds. The quads were born after the five-year-old animal had been artificially inseminated.

* * *

Rags was considered the town dog at Kokomo. For nineteen years it was the pet of a small business center on the south side of town. When the dog was killed in traffic, the body was embalmed, placed in a white box covered with flowers, and lay in state on the street corner the dog had loved. The funeral on July 14, 1942, stopped traffic; the businesses closed half an hour during Rags's eulogy.

■ INFANTILE INCIDENTS

The son born January 19, 1937, to Mr. and Mrs. Elmer Fleck of Ari, near Fort Wayne, weighed seventeen pounds, four ounces, one of the largest babies ever born in Indiana and among the largest ever documented in America. The child, the fifth in the Fleck family, was delivered by Dr. Jesse Briggs of Churubusco.

Medical authorities said that a baby heavier than fifteen pounds occurred only once every 250,000 births.

But the Fleck baby had another outstanding feature. It was named Franklin because Franklin D. Roosevelt had just been inaugurated, and this telegraph in the child's name was sent to FDR: "As one big man to another, I offer my sincere congratulations. I was named for you, which honor I greatly appreciate."

*   *   *

At James Whitcomb Riley Hospital in December 1972, when the child of an Anderson couple was brought in for examination, a tumor-like object was detected in the baby's stomach. Dr. Jay Grosfeld operated and removed the object.

Chromosome examination showed that it was an undeveloped identical male twin.

"There are only ten or eleven such cases in recorded history," said Dr. Grosfeld, "and only half of those cases have been fully documented. Medical science is not sure exactly how this occurs."

Authorities did not reveal the names of the child's parents.

THE BROTHERS OF STONE ■

It started when Charles Richard Wagner was in grade school. He fell and broke his leg.

Schooling for the boy ended in grade 2B. Death came on January 16, 1937, when Wagner was eighteen.

He had turned to stone.

Family, friends, and neighbors in Muncie watched helplessly through the years as Wagner's flesh slowly hardened into an almost stonelike condition. Physicians were baffled. They came from all over the country to examine Charles. Some thought a deficiency—perhaps a lack of calcium—was causing a kind of ossification.

Suggested remedies came from around the world. But the hardening was relentless. Wagner's muscles became rigid. Gradually he lost the use of his arms and legs. By the time of his death, Charles was immobile except for slight movement in one arm.

His parents, Mr. and Mrs. Murray Wagner, and a sister, Mrs. Edna McLaughlin, who lived at Daleville, were physically normal.

But Charles's brother, William, was undergoing the same transformation. When Charles died, William, eleven, attended his brother's funeral in a wheelchair. Already his muscles were so hard he could not get around on his own.

Strangely, William seemed to drop from sight after the funeral. Muncie newspapers provide no information on what happened to him and medical journals at the Indiana University School of Medicine in Indianapolis give no mention of William Wagner.

But, considering the state of medical science in the 1930s and the fact that doctors were certain William's case was hopeless, it is probable that he became the second Wagner to die by hardening into stone.

■ Music to Milk By

When the word of what Almond Wickard was doing with his two cows hit the press, he became an agricultural celebrity.

Wickard was the Hancock County road superintendent who tried something new; he put a radio in the cow barn. The discovery that his cows gave more milk when the radio played made news from coast to coast. Wickard received clippings from as far away as Waterbury, Connecticut, when the story began circulating in January 1937.

A California newspaper dubbed the cows Cleopatra and Mary Queen of Scots. Milk production was tied to bovine likes and dislikes. Two buckets of milk for Major Bowes, three for Jack Benny, but for Bob Burns and his bazooka, umpteen buckets—the milk just flowed like water.

"If somebody could only invent a radio," the article concluded, "that would wind the clock and put out the cat, we would all move to the country."

■ Wanted: One Model

If you've ever wondered about the identity of the person who looked like Uncle Sam and said "I Want You" in the famous World War II poster, he was Walter Botts of Sullivan.

Botts posed for artist James Montgomery Flagg, who

painted the poster in 1938. A saxophonist and band vocalist at night, Botts modeled for billboard ads and magazine covers by day. A New York modeling agency sent him to Flagg's studio. Two others had also applied.

"He picked me from the three mainly, I think, because of my bushy eyebrow and long nose," Botts recalled in 1971. "I spent three days sitting for him. He tried to figure out what I should do with my arms. I suggested pointing my finger as if to say I want you."

Botts, who played with Jack Teagarden, Johnny Johnson, Red Nichols, and Harry James, died August 9, 1972, at the age of seventy-two.

THE VILLAGE THAT VANISHED ■

Indiana lost one complete town because of World War II.

Wiped out without casualties was a miniature village of make-believe called Littleville, built from 1937 to 1941 on four lots in Chesterton.

A tourist attraction which gained national attention, Littleville was closed by wartime shortages and the need to conserve electricity. It never reopened. Its buildings met various fates until only a single castle survives in the back yard of Robert C. Johnson.

Littleville was created by William Murray, spurred by sale of birdhouses he built and public admiration of a small structure he made for a restaurant.

Using bricks made of concrete and shingles cut from wood and linoleum, he built homes, churches, filling stations, a seventy-five-foot-long railroad, a miniature of the Cerro Gordo County courthouse in Mason City, Iowa, a model of Neuschwanstein Castle in Bavaria. There were oil bulk storage tanks, a sewage treatment plant, a movie theater, a Ferris wheel in the park, and tiny Burma Shave

Robert C. Johnson in his back yard at Chesterton shows off the castle that is the only structure left from Littleville, the village that vanished. (Photo by the author)

signs. Buildings were lighted. Some churches had sound coming from inside.

Jewel Cadet Paint advertised that three and a half gallons of its paint had covered an entire town. An insurance company boasted of covering an entire community with one policy. Sinclair Oil Corporation filmed Littleville to show off the tiny gasoline station bearing a Sinclair sign.

Neighborhood children paid a nickel to tour the town. They got a copy of the *Littleville News* for two cents.

Popularity increased. In 1938 a total of 20,000 visitors came; by 1940 the annual visits had reached 50,000.

Now, except for the castle, Littleville is gone, obliterated by a war which not only curtailed materials, but also somehow stemmed the incentive of its creator.

ODON'S HOME FIRES BURNING ■

Fires of uncertain origin have fascinated and frightened people for ages, but the leading Indiana incident of baffling blazes would be the twenty-eight fires at Odon which not only puzzled observers but pushed a family out of its home forever.

A few minute before 8:00 A.M. in April 1941, smoke was smelled in the home of William Hackler and his family near Odon. Investigation showed a fire inside the wall of a bedroom.

The house was not wired for electricity, but the family had no time to contemplate this; they called the Odon fire department. No sooner was that fire under control than the firemen had to return for another fire in a mattress in another bedroom.

Between 8:00 and 11:00 A.M., nine fires in all were discovered. No causes could be found and all members of the family swore they had nothing to do with the blazes.

One fireman noticed smoke on a shelf, took down a book, and found it burning inside. A pair of Hackler's coveralls hanging behind a door burned and neighbors saw a bedspread ignite; a calendar on the kitchen wall burst into flames.

The house itself never caught fire; damage was generally limited to the flaming items themselves.

For Hackler it was a burnout. Beds were moved outside so the family could sleep under the stars. Then he dismantled the house and used the material to build another dwelling several miles away.

By all accounts, Hackler's new home never experienced a rash of fires and, by all accounts, nobody ever pinpointed the reason for the blazes. Some blamed magnetism. Others said gas from a well might have been to blame.

The event did benefit the Traveler's Insurance Company. On April 19, 1941, the firm described the Hackler fires in an advertisement in *Collier's* magazine, with the boast that it had carried the insurance—against fires from any source, no matter how mysterious.

■ THE ATTACK BLIMP

The only American blimp lost during World War II was piloted by a Hoosier who never had received training in tactics, never before had dropped a bomb, and was at his location because of a flip of a coin. When it turned out that the German submarine encountered off Florida was the first in those waters equipped with antiaircraft guns, the elements of an unprecedented drama were complete.

Nelson Grills, reared in Hammond and later an attorney in Indianapolis, got a Purple Heart for the action instead of a court-martial, which was first threatened.

On July 14, 1943, Lieutenant Grills, who had been piloting a blimp for only a few months, left the Richmond Naval Air Station near Miami with another blimp whose pilot had flipped a coin with Grills. As a result of the coin flip, Grills headed toward the Keys on regular submarine patrol and the other blimp headed north toward Palm Beach.

When Grills spotted a submarine about midnight, he decided to attack instead of wait for help because he knew U.S. tankers were due soon from the north. "I figured losing one blimp was cheaper than two tankers," he said later.

He dropped two depth charges, something he never had done in training, and the sub answered with shots that put holes in the envelope of the blimp. It sagged and settled on the water.

Grills stayed in the water near the blimp to guard its equipment and was rescued twenty hours later by a submarine chaser. Eight of the other nine crew members had been picked up by another blimp hours earlier. One man drowned.

After a hospital stay, Grills was assigned to supervise blimp training exercises in the Atlantic. Only years later did he learn that the submarine he attacked had been damaged, had headed back to Germany, and had been sunk by the British in the English Channel.

BITTEN BY FAME ■

So it was a Friday the 13th. And what the eighteen-month-old child thought was a black kitty turned out to be a skunk, which probably was rabid. It seized Linda Lukens by three fingers on the left hand and her father, after beating the animal to death, had to pry its teeth from her flesh. She could have lost three fingers on that August 13, 1943. Instead she found a career.

Linda, who lived on a farm six miles northeast of Rochester, made many Hoosier newspapers as the child unlucky enough to be bitten by a rabid skunk on Friday the 13th. She was further unlucky; because her father had destroyed the skunk's brain in killing it, no rabies test could be made. Linda and her father had to take a painful series of anti-rabies shots.

With all this attention, plus the fact that she was as cute a child as ever was bitten by a skunk, Linda came to the attention of Chicago model agencies. Soon she was listed with the Chicago Models Bureau.

Linda's first job was posing for an illustration used on May 29, 1945, in the *Chicago Tribune*. That job, which earned her $2.50 an hour, brought her more publicity. She became the youngest person in Indiana at that time to have a Social Security card.

Soon she was chosen to be the Quaker Oats girl for a series of advertisements in *Life, Look, Farm Journal, Woman's Day, Pathfinder, Ladies Home Journal,* and *McCalls.* She modeled for the Sears, Roebuck 1945 Christmas catalog and for the Marshall Field store in Chicago. Linda's face appeared in ads in *Nation's Business, Newsweek, Time, Saturday Evening Post, American Home,* and *Popular Photography.* She could be seen in ads in streetcars and buses and on billboards.

She played children's roles on the Chicago stage. She was chosen in 1947 to star in a campaign by Sears to inspire politeness among its employees. A film featuring Linda carried the courtesy campaign to Sears stores all over the U.S. and South America.

In October 1948, Linda made her television debut on WBKB in Chicago on the program *Let's Play School.* She got $7 a show.

In 1951, just before her tenth birthday, Linda won top prize in the popular Morris B. Sacks Amateur Hour doing impressions of celebrities like Jimmy Durante, Tallulah Bankhead, and Marilyn Monroe.

The last modeling job Linda did as a child was for Toni permanents.

As a teen-ager she won a 4-H contest which brought her a trip to New York to be interviewed by Dave Garroway on the old "Today" show. In 1960 she was runner-up to Miss Indiana and crowned National Pork Queen.

What happened to Linda after that was that she grew up. But it was a fast ride for a child while it lasted.

And all because a rabid skunk bit her on Friday the 13th.

Among the strangest tales ever told by Frank Edwards, a radio and television news commentator in Bloomington and Indianapolis noted for strange yarns, was the one about the psychic horse.

The incident involved Ronnie Weitcamp, three years old, who disappeared about noon on October 11, 1955, in the acres of woods around the Crane Naval Depot (now the Crane Naval Weapons Support Center) in south-central Indiana.

Search parties were unsuccessful after eleven days and it was not known whether he had wandered away or been kidnapped.

Edwards, then news director of television station WTTV in Bloomington, asked a friend on the East Coast to travel 175 miles to Richmond, Virginia, to consult Lady Wonder, the horse with ESP. Lady Wonder, authorities claimed, had directed them to a site in Massachusetts where the body of a missing boy had been found. Maybe she could do it again, Edwards thought.

The horse answered questions by flipping over tin letters on a bar across her stall. Edwards's friend, who never has been identified, sought out the thirty-five-year-old horse and began getting answers to inquiries.

Was Ronnie dead? Dead. Kidnapped? No. Where would he be found? In a hole. More than a quarter mile but less than a mile from where he had been seen last? Yes. What is near him? Elm. Soil? Sand. When will he be found? December. That's what the man said the horse said.

It was only what believers in Lady Wonder would have expected. She had been able to count and spell out words by the time she was two years old. Her fame spread. She sometimes did math for visitors, who paid fifty cents a question. She predicted that Franklin D. Roosevelt would be the next president of the United States—even before he was nominated. Fourteen times in seventeen years she had predicted the winner of the World Series. She easily predicted the winners of horse races—as might be expected—until her owner, a Mrs. Fonda, stopped accepting such questions.

On October 24, 1955, Edwards broadcast Lady Wonder's message about the Ronnie Weitcamp case and got the expected horse laughs.

But when the boy's body was found—on December 4—Edwards reported that the circumstances were very close to what the horse had foreseen. The boy had died of exposure about a mile from where he disappeared, his body was in sandy soil, and an elm tree was nearby.

Which leaves one to wonder what might have happened if Lady Wonder had been interrogated immediately after the child disappeared. But that is hindsight instead of ESP.

■ A Salute to the Kernel

When you combine a major Indiana crop and some of its kings with Hoosier pride and a flair for the dramatic, it is easy to see why Shelbyville did it. Some say it was the most beautiful corn shock ever constructed. And some are certain it was the biggest.

The shock soared seventy feet tall, the centerpiece for the Shelby County Corn Festival in October 1956.

The shock had a large utility pole as its center. Steel guy wires from near the top of the pole anchored it to concrete on the ground. Wire mesh panels were covered with an estimated 10,000 corn stalks which were hoisted onto the framework. At least 200 4-H members and their leaders helped assemble the shock in the Shelbyville town square.

Shelby County had the heritage for it. In 1919 Peter Lux was named national corn king. He repeated in 1922, 1926, and 1934, and other Lux family members earned the crown over a number of years. Ed Lux won in 1931. Frank Lux won in 1953 and 1959; Maurice Lux in 1960; Charles Fischer, also of Shelby County, won corn king crowns in 1940, 1949, 1950, 1957, and 1963.

The shock was a suitable salute to people like the Lux family and others involved in Shelby County's perennial dominance in corn production and seed corn output. The shock was the brainchild of Art Chafee, a professional photographer in Shelbyville.

Ronald W. Reagan, then a special promotional representative of the General Electric Company, visited Shelbyville about ten days before the festival opened and was photographed in front of the shock. He also made several speeches. The festival featured a talent show in the Shelbyville High School gymnasium with television personality Jack Paar as master of ceremonies.

It was an impressive festival even for a county where corn was king. There have been other corn festivals, but there never was anything to equal the seventy-foot shock.

Ring around the Commode ■

When Robert Kemp of Munster lost his 1960 class ring in the toilet of a grocery store on the South Side of Chicago he was devastated but helpless. He had only had the ring from Mount Carmel Catholic High School in Chicago for two weeks before he dropped it in the toilet tank and watched it disappear down the overflow pipe.

It was gone forever, he concluded.

Later, a medic in Vietnam told Kemp that the ring probably was still in the toilet trap. Kemp, who often passed that old grocery while commuting from Munster to his Chicago insurance job, noticed in February 1987 that a demolition crew was working on the site. If the toilet still was intact, could he look in it for his ring, Kemp asked.

Dubious workmen quickly became convinced of his sincerity by an offer of $100 if the ring were found. It was, by workman Tyrone Rogers, who smashed the toilet with a hammer.

After twenty-seven years of flushing the ring was back on Kemp's finger.

■ No Bones about It

Young Robert Swarts thought he was lucky—as lucky as you can be when your motorcycle and a semi-trailer truck collide head-on. His accident on a Marion street left him with an obviously fractured leg and a cut less than 2 inches long just above the left knee. Swarts was treated for shock, three stitches closed the cut, a splint was applied to the leg.

Then they developed the X-rays.

Dr. B., as he has insisted on being identified, found that Swarts's upper leg bone—the largest bone in the human body—was gone.

"There was no way for that bone to have gotten out except through the tiny cut above Swarts's knee, and that appeared to be entirely too small to allow a bone the size of a femur to puncture it and escape," he said.

Then police found a seven and a half inch section of bone wedged between the truck bumper and a supporting brace. It had been split lengthwise. Dr. B put it in a chloride solution. In twenty-five years of practice, including two years as a combat surgeon in the South Pacific, he had seen nothing like this. And he was in largely unexplored territory. Transplants and replacements were not routine in 1962.

Next day a mechanic brought in another piece of bone, found embedded under a fender of the truck.

On the third day Dr. B. scrubbed and sterilized both bone sections. Then he brought Swarts back to reality. Surgery was the only answer if Swarts were to walk again. Nine days after the accident, surgeons inserted a rod in Swarts's thigh, set the bone sections in place, and attached them to the rod.

Three months later Swarts could walk on crutches.

Further surgery repaired some kneecap damage. After eight months, Swarts was mobile on crutches. Twenty-two months after the accident he took his first step without crutches.

Dr. B. removed the rod two and a half years after the surgery. The bones had knitted.

Swarts fully recovered; twenty years later, well into his fifties, he could do everything he did before the accident—except ride a motorcycle.

"I can't bend my leg back far enough," he explained.

Replacing bones may be routine today. But what still is hard to explain is how the largest bone in the body could escape through a two-inch cut, not to be reunited with the leg until nine days later.

Test Case for Auctioneers ■

The Skiles Edward Test auction in Indianapolis was one of the largest—and strangest—in Indiana history.

Test, one of the richest men in the Midwest and certainly one of the region's strangest millionaires, left behind an estate which once had included twenty buildings and had kept thirty employees busy.

It took eight days to prepare Test's household effects for auction. The sale was May 21–24, 1964, slightly more than two months after Test's death at the age of seventy-four.

Just getting a peek at the legendary estate in northeast Marion County was enough to attract many. However, not even the auctioneers were prepared for the estimated 50,000 who attended the sale. A first-aid station was established and the firemen were on duty. What the auction-goers saw verified many of the lurid tales about the millionaire and his self-sufficiency on the estate around his home, known as the House of Blue Lights. This appellation came from the blue Christmas lights Test left up all year at the house. In their eerie blue glow, a glimpse of someone sleeping is believed to have been the source of the false story that Test kept his dead wife in a coffin in the house.

If this story was untrue, there were still plenty of odd elements in the lifestyle developed by Test with wealth inherited from his father, supplemented by investment property. He had his own water tower, sawmill, a home-made generating plant, a pipe system to heat 100,000 gallons of water for the forty-by-eighty-foot pool, a cemetery for the many cats which had died after a lifetime in Test's kennel equipped with small heated houses. There also were graves of dogs, squirrels, and birds.

The auction crowd explored a basement consisting of dark storage rooms connected by a labyrinth of passageways. One room held liquor, another milk bottles, another fruit and wine, etc.

There was a baby grand player piano and 150 rolls of music for it. There were nine vehicles, 15,000 records (used for automatic consoles which piped music to loudspeakers around the swimming pool), $75,000 worth of hardware items, 300 bottles of aspirin, 150 kegs of new nails, several hundred tons of junk. There were bales of twine, cases of canned food, thousands of plumbing and electrical parts.

Missing were any bottles of catsup from a railroad car full which Test had purchased before World War II. Employees said he had consumed the last bottle of catsup three months before he died.

In 1974, in accordance with his will, the Test estate was given to the city in hopes it would become a park, although by 1989 this had not occurred. In 1978 the house was razed, the final scene in the tale and sale of Indiana's oddest millionaire.

EXECUTION BY SURGERY ■

The cause of death for condemned Hoosier murderer Emmett O. Hashfield was not the electric chair, as Indiana officials had planned, but a tonsillectomy. At the time of his death the sixty-six-year-old prison inmate had evaded electrocution for twelve years on technicalities.

Hashfield was convicted in 1962 in Bloomington of the brutal sex murder of eleven-year-old Avril Terry of Boonville. Although sentenced to death, various technicalities postponed the electrocution. For one thing, debates over the morality of the death penalty were gaining steam. For another, he and his attorneys contended they were not present in court when the death penalty was assessed. Courts heard a series of debates about violation of his rights.

The original death date of July 1, 1968, passed. On January 10, 1974, Hashfield was taken from Indiana State Prison at Michigan City to nearby St. Anthony Hospital for a tonsillectomy. Complications ensued, and he died February 2 of uncontrolled bleeding.

Not only was his death not reported to the public for nearly a week, his body wasn't claimed either. It was finally released to the Indiana University Medical Center in Indianapolis without religious rites.

■ THE FALL AND RISE OF ROGER REYNOLDS

The fact that Roger Reynolds of Indianapolis fell about 2,000 feet to the ground and lived is startling. But not as remarkable as the fact that, four years after that fall, he successfully ran the Boston Marathon.

Reynolds joined the Army in 1971 when he was eighteen and wound up on the Golden Knights skydiving team performing one of the hit acts of the show. He would jump from a plane, open one parachute, glide downward, then cut that chute and appear to be falling chuteless. At the last safe moment, he would open a second chute and settle safely on the ground.

On April 24, 1974, during a performance at the Dogwood Festival at Charlottesville, Virginia, he jumped from about 2,000 feet, his 960th career jump. His first chute came out, but the silk did not open. The second chute got tangled in the first.

"I was about 1,000 feet from the ground when I realized I was going to die," he said later.

Landing on his left side at an estimated eighty miles an hour, Reynolds suffered extensive fractures to his left shoulder, ribs, hip, pelvis, arm, leg, ankle, and heel. He was bleeding severely.

He survived, he believes, because of his good physical condition, because he did not land on his feet, and because he landed in the yard of a physician who got to him immediately.

At the University of Virginia Hospital he was in traction four months. He was hospitalized twelve months and in casts a total of fourteen months.

Back in Indianapolis, studying medicine at Indiana

University–Purdue University, Indianapolis, Reynolds decided in September 1976, to start jogging, although doctors had said he could never and should never run again.

By May 1977, he was able to run in the thirteen-mile Indy Mini-Marathon, finishing in the top third.

On April 17, 1978, Reynolds finished the Boston Marathon in three hours and forty-six minutes and he knew he had risen further than he had fallen.

THE POSTER THAT SHOULDN'T HAVE BEEN ■

Rodney Brown of Noblesville was chosen as Indiana's cystic fibrosis poster child in 1975, five years after he had been diagnosed as having the usually fatal respiratory illness. The next year Rodney was chosen national poster child by the Cystic Fibrosis Foundation and, in that role, posed with President Gerald Ford. There was only one problem with this sequence of events. Luckily for Rodney, he never had cystic fibrosis.

The truth became known in 1980 after the Browns moved to Maryland, where a test conducted at Johns Hopkins Hospital in Baltimore showed Rodney did not have the ailment. Two follow-up tests at Children's Hospital in Washington, D.C., and at the National Institutes of Health in Bethesda, Maryland, confirmed that finding.

"He never had C.F." said Dr. Van S. Hubbard, a specialist at the National Institutes of Health. "He had a recurring respiratory disease which was diagnosed as C.F. and he has been treated as a C.F. patient, but he is not cystic."

Instead of facing almost certain death by the age of twenty, Rodney could expect a normal life.

Rodney's original diagnosis had been made at Methodist Hospital in Indianapolis. Specialists believe classic symptoms of cystic fibrosis in the fifteen-month-old boy were due to an asthmatic condition and pneumonia. Those problems may have resulted in abnormal perspiration, hampered breathing, and digestive difficulty, all indications of cystic fibrosis.

Rodney's father, Harold L. Brown, said that when the boy was told he didn't have cystic fibrosis—although he had undergone ten years of X rays, taking antibiotics, and undergoing physical and inhalation therapy—he commented: "I got to see the President for free."

■ MARJORIE'S MILLIONS

Tales about eccentric elderly widows and widowers are legion, but surely one of the strangest is the story of Marjorie Jackson. Her eccentricity came to light in May 1976, when a burglar took $800,000 from her northside Indianapolis home and she declined to press charges against a captured suspect. A prosecutor's aide and some deputy sheriffs went to talk to the sixty-six-year-old widow about the burglary. She met them in her nightgown, armed with what later turned out to be a cap gun, and ordered them to leave.

A year later, on May 7, 1977, her body was discovered by firemen called to investigate a fire on her property. She had been shot with a .22 caliber pistol. Harold Young and Harlan Rynard, two sheriff's sergeants, found a plastic garbage can full of $100 bills in a bedroom closet. They started counting but stopped when they reached $700,000, deciding to call a higher-ranking deputy.

Gradually the details of Marjorie Jackson's lifestyle became known. It began when her husband, Chester Jackson, owner of the Standard Grocery Company chain, died in 1970, leaving her $9 million. "The shock of losing him really cracked her," one neighbor explained. She erected a chain-link fence around her three-acre property, allowed the weeds to form a barrier against the outside, and ordered deliverymen to blow the horn and pass parcels to her over the fence.

The Bible occupied her attention; her schedule included four days a week for meditation and playing the organ. "Demons" were warded off by placing aluminum foil around the doorknobs. The death of shrubbery was blamed on the devil. She feared going out only slightly more than staying home. A broken water hose on her old Cadillac prompted her to buy two new Sevilles for $27,000. One of them was still unlicensed when investigators appeared.

Fear that her bank was cheating her led her to begin withdrawing money from her accounts. This prompted Indiana National Bank to seek guardianship rights in February 1976. But when it was found that a bank official had in fact embezzled $700,000 from her trust fund, Mrs. Jackson was allowed to retain control of her finances. She continued drawing money out, sometimes as much as $500,000 at a time.

When firemen arrived to investigate the fire on that May morning, they found Mrs. Jackson's body in her kitchen, a bullet wound in the stomach. Nearly $5 million was found all over the house—in a garbage can, tool boxes, drawers, and vacuum cleaners. Furs hung in the garage. A freezer was full of cheese. The table was set as for a banquet. Scattered all about were cakes and gift-wrapped packages containing small items like washcloths, bearing tags that read "To Jesus Christ from Marjorie Jackson" and "To God from Marjorie."

Within a month, two men were apprehended. They had called attention to themselves by going on a wild spending spree. Manuel Lee Robinson, eventually convicted of burglary, had $1.6 million from the Jackson home. His partner in the crime, Howard "Billy Joe" Willard, was convicted of murder, burglary, and arson. Willard's ex-wife led FBI agents to another $1.7 million buried in the Arizona desert. In all, police recovered $4 million believed taken from the Jackson house. Authorities estimate $6 million was taken, the largest amount of money ever taken in an American burglary.

The irony was, police said, that the two men had committed a crime almost impossible to solve and then left a trail almost impossible to miss. Had they not set fire to the house, the body of the recluse might not have been discovered for weeks. And if they had not wildly and irrationally started spending the money, they might easily have lived the rest of their lives on it. An investigator said the execution of the crime was "so colossally stupid" that one of the perpetrators spent most of his time in prison evading the ridicule of his fellow inmates.

What happened to the house? It was sold to Helen M. Corwin, another eccentric widow—as the neighbors soon discovered. Because she was opposed to cutting the lawn, the local neighborhood association took her to court in an attempt to have the place spruced up. A few years later Indianapolis attorney Robert Thompson was named Mrs. Corwin's limited guardian.

Coincidentally, it was not Thompson's first connection with the Jackson house. He had been the prosecutor's aide ordered off the place at the point of a cap gun when he tried to get Mrs. Jackson to prosecute the burglar who took $800,000. If Mrs. Jackson had followed his advice that time, the bizarre events might never have happened.

■ A Home That's Quite a House

Indiana's oddest house sits on a hillside off Indiana 46 west of Spencer.

It has thirty-two rooms with 7,240 square feet of floor space. No two rooms are the same size or shape, and no two rooms are perpendicular to each other. The house is 135 feet long and rises seventy feet in four or five levels to the top of twin towers. It has fifteen stairways and ladders. There are three chimneys containing 3,000 · bricks. There are seventy-four different roof angles.

And hardly any material used in the house was new. Jim Pendleton, who built the house in ten years, beginning in 1972, used materials from eleven barns and seven houses which he razed.

The Barn House, as he calls it, catches the eye of an estimated twenty motorists a week; Pendleton gladly gives tours to those who stop when he is at home. He also holds an annual festival the first weekend of October so those who haven't had a chance can tour the Barn House.

In three years 3,200 visitors signed Pendleton's guest book, showing addresses from as far away as Japan, Thai-

Pendleton's one-of-a-kind house west of Spencer has thirty-two rooms. The startling landmark is seventy feet tall. (Photo by the author)

land, India, Russia, Vietnam, Czechoslovakia, and Afghanistan.

"Everybody," explained Pendleton, "has his own style of doing something different."

■ MOTHER PLAYED BASKETBALL

Denise Jackson was one of the key players for the Indiana University women's basketball team which shared the Big Ten championship in 1983. She was named to the All–Big Ten team, was a regional All-American, and was named I.U. Woman Athlete of the Year. She was also pregnant.

Denise was about four months from delivery of a baby girl when the I.U. season ended. The child, Meesha LaShonda Jackson, was born August 30, 1983.

After first considering abortion, Denise decided to play pregnant with the support and monitoring of her coach, the team physician, and the team trainer. Few others knew about the pregnancy.

Although there were some nervous moments, Denise did not suffer any physical problems. Near the end of the season she was named Big Ten Player of the Week for a two-game road trip in which she scored a total of fifty-one points and got thirty-five rebounds against Iowa and Minnesota.

In the National Collegiate Athletic Association tournament, Denise scored twenty-three points and got eleven rebounds as I.U. beat Kentucky. She scored twenty-five points and got twelve rebounds as the I.U. team lost the next week to Georgia, putting Indiana out of the tournament.

Denise spent the summer of 1983 at the Bloomington campus and gave birth in Bloomington Hospital on the first day of fall semester classes.

The team trainer, Sue Hannam, summarized the unusual basketball season: "How many kids can grow up saying, 'I won a Big Ten championship with my mother?'"

FISH STORIES ■

They thought Ralph Daum told tall tales. He was a bartender at the Patio Restaurant which he operated between Tell City and Cannelton, after all, and was prone to harmless exaggeration like many bartenders.

But investigation showed that Daum had trained fish in the small lake at his home to come when he whistled twice. The whistle caused the water close to shore to boil with hungry fish and some would slither onto the muddy bank in their rush to dinner.

Bluegills and hefty catfish would take commercial fish food from Daum's hands.

Frank Etherton's pet bass rises to take a night crawler offered by Wanda Cavinder. (Photo by the author)

"You have to work with fish a little more than you would another creature, but they can be trained and they can become your friends," Daum told a reporter.

*   *   *

North of Madison, Frank Etherton taught his pet bass to come when a light pole was kicked beside a small pond.

The fish would wait for Etherton to hold a worm near the top of the water. Then the fish would break the surface, seize the worm, and plunge back under, spinning at once to be in position for another worm.

Given the fish by an angler, Etherton first tossed food to the bass and gradually altered the feeding until the bass would take worms from his fingers.

Sex of the bass was uncertain. But, male or female, it ruled the waves in Jefferson County for about five years until an unidentified and unwelcome angler caught it one night in the summer of 1989. The demise of the bass left Frank Etherton in mourning for his pet but with his reputation untarnished as a fish tamer on an unprecedented scale.

■ WETTING DAY

Brendt L. Smith, a Warsaw insurance salesman, swam across fifty-two lakes in Kosciusko County in eighteen hours and twenty-eight minutes, crossing a total of sixteen miles of water.

The effort began at 5:30 A.M. on Labor Day, 1986 and ended at 11:18 P.M. Smith traveled 150 miles by automobile to reach the lakes. His swim was not only a record attempt, but also raised money in memory of his father, John Smith, who had died of cancer in 1984.

The largest lake, Wawasee, was 5,400 feet wide where Smith crossed it in a thirty-two minute swim. The smallest lakes he swam were Schultz, Reed, and Moorehead, each 500 feet across. His fastest time for a 500-foot lake was one minute and forty-five seconds.

Two by Two by Two ■

The odds against it happening are 100,000 to 1.

But Lynnville in Warrick County beat the odds in 1986.

The town with a population of slightly more than 600 had three sets of twins born to residents within forty-six days.

Dr. Robert Calhoun, director of public health statistics at the Indiana Board of Health, calculated the odds for a community of that size, but could not even make a guess at the odds of it all occurring within about six weeks.

The first set of twins was born on February 22 to Bob and Connie McCleland. The twins were named Felicia Nicole and Kyle Thomas. On April 5, twins were born to Gordon and Susan Wood. They were named Lisa May and Katherine Lynn. Four days later, B.J. and Jammie Siebe became the parents of twins Brady McClain and Jordon Scot.

All three families had one older child when the twins were born. Twins were not in the history of any of the parents of the couples or their grandparents. None of the parents of the twins had any siblings.

The nonscientific conclusion some people in Lynnville arrived at was that it must have been something in the water.

■ A Little Soft Soap Never Hurt

Eiffel G. Plasterer was forever blowing bubbles.

He blew them large enough to surround a person; he produced bubbles that climbed and bounced and bubbles which appeared inside other bubbles. He kept some bubbles intact for years and once carried one from Indiana to the West Coast for a show.

His forty-five years of researching soap film phenomena brought him appearances on such television shows as "Ripley's Believe It or Not" and "That's Incredible," and prompted Huntington, his home town, to name a street in his honor.

In April 1986, when he was eighty-six, Huntington announced that the next street built in the town would be named Plasterer Avenue—a more permanent memorial than bubbles.

"You name a street after someone, it's there," said one city official. Plasterer had taught physics and chemistry at Huntington High School and at Huntington College. He died in 1989.

■ In the Chips

Most people see in potato chips only the capacity for munching or dipping. But Myrtle Young of Fort Wayne has spotted more than two hundred chips which look like something else, such as people, birds, and cowboy boots.

An inspector for Seyfert Foods Inc., she began collecting potato chip lookalikes in mid-1987. She found chips that look like Mr. Magoo, Bob Hope, Rodney Dangerfield and Yogi Bear, although Yogi regrettably broke. She collected four sets of chips that resemble twin brothers.

Rescued from among normal chips as they pass by Mrs. Young on a conveyor belt, the collectibles are put on newspaper to dry naturally in the air.

When transported to television shows at Fort Wayne, Cincinnati, "The Tonight Show Starring Johnny Carson," or "Late Night with David Letterman," the chips are placed in plastic containers on pillows of cotton batting.

Museums have sought the chips, but Mrs. Young discounts any lasting fame.

"I've said I'm going to wake up some morning and my car's going to turn into a pumpkin," she said.

A pumpkin, no doubt, which looks to her like something else.

BEATING THE ODDS ■

A common bacteria that most people are exposed to every day cost Paul Geyman of Madison both arms, both legs, his lips, part of his nose, part of his tongue, and large sections of his skin—all because of a missing spleen. Yet Geyman survived against all medical logic.

"I don't know of anyone with a case this extreme who lived," said Dr. Michael Niemeier, who treated Geyman at Methodist Hospital in Indianapolis.

Geyman, thirty-three, lost his spleen as the result of an auto accident on Valentine's Day, 1973. When he developed an infection on March 4, 1987, due to common pneumococcal bacteria, which usually cause simple cold-like symptoms, he quickly became so ill he was flown from Madison to Indianapolis. There he suffered multiple organ failure and had to be hooked to a life-support system.

After Geyman survived three weeks of illness and the amputations, he was vaccinated to help prevent further infections.

By mid-June he was well enough to be transferred to the Rehabilitation Institute of Chicago to begin adaptation of artificial limbs and training to use a wheel chair.

Doctors credited Geyman's survival to his youth and mental strength. "Most people that sick just go ahead and die," said Dr. Niemeier.

FRED D. CAVINDER is the author of *The Indiana Book of Records, Firsts, and Fascinating Facts*. He is a graduate of Indiana University and for over thirty years has been a reporter for *The Indianapolis Star* and editor of the *Star Magazine* for sixteen years. His photographs and articles have appeared in numerous regional, state, and international publications.